AN
AMERICAN
at WAR

ii

ISBN 979-8-218-56455-1

Siggy Schreiner in uniform.

BATAAN DEATH MARCH
APRIL 9–17, 1942

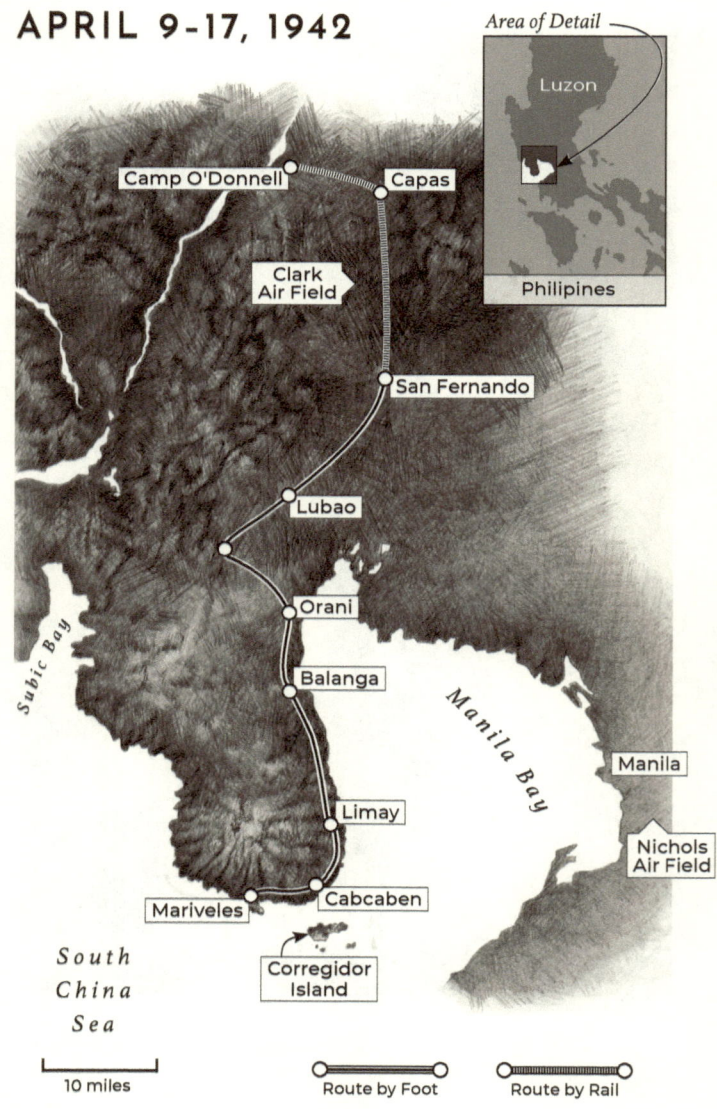

Area of Detail

Luzon

Philipines

Camp O'Donnell — Capas

Clark
Air Field

San Fernando

Lubao

Orani

Balanga

Manila

Nichols
Air Field

Manila Bay

Limay

Subic Bay

Mariveles — Cabcaben

Corregidor
Island

South
China
Sea

10 miles

Route by Foot   Route by Rail

SIGGY *in the* PACIFIC

1941-1945

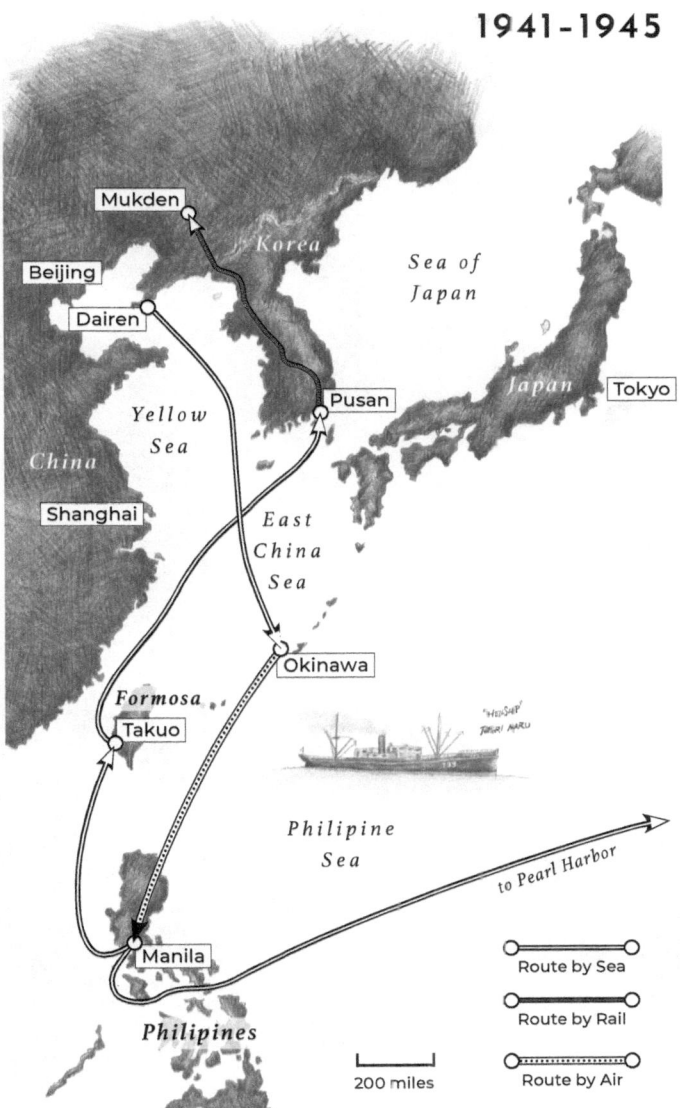

AN
AMERICAN
at WAR

—▬—

Surviving Bataan, Mukden,
and the Trauma of Recovery

Siggy as a gymnast *(left)*.

When she died in 1993 only eight months shy of her hundredth birthday, Josepha Rogan Schreiner might well have been the last person on the planet—at least on this side of the Atlantic—who had seen the Austrian Emperor Franz Joseph in the flesh. She remembered the white whiskers, the medals, the slight stoop.

Memory is always unstable. My grandmother's recollection was off in one regard: the location. She believed she had watched the eighty-three-year-old Habsburg ruler and his entourage exiting the cathedral in Milan where she was working at the time, but there isn't any record of the Emperor's unlikely presence in Italy then. The eighteen-year-old Josepha, having fled the tedium of the farm where she grew up in the north of Slovenia (then a part of the

Austro-Hungarian Empire), had found a job through a family friend as a dining-room hostess at a hotel in Milan that catered to German-speaking guests. Her glimpse of Austria's aging Kaiser, though, was more likely to have been in Vienna, possibly outside St. Stephen's Cathedral or the *Karlskirche*. The year was 1912.

Several months after her return home, Josepha gave in to her younger sister Antoinette's importunities to join her and some Rogan cousins in emigrating to the United States. The family knew people in a city near Hartford, Connecticut, who told them of better prospects, greater freedom, and a vibrant German and Austrian community. Josepha hesitated, briefly, but then decided to make the crossing. What future was there on a farm in the countryside with a doting father and a mother who was anything but doting?

The sisters' timing was spectacularly fortuitous. Josepha and Antoinette were safely out of Europe in 1913 before the Emperor's nephew and heir apparent, Franz Ferdinand, and his wife made their famous, misguided, and tragic visit to Sarajevo in the summer of 1914. They were spared what the rest of their family was not: seeing their brothers drafted into the Austrian army and sent off to fight in an apocalyptic war that year (resulting in the death of over a million soldiers of the Austro-Hungarian Empire), the death of the old Emperor in 1916, the Allied victory, the collapse of the economy, and the widespread famine that ensued. They were likewise spared the later

incorporation of their village into the newly formed
nation of Yugoslavia, the annexation of Austria into
Hitler's Reich, and the Russian invasion of the region
to drive the Nazis out in 1945.

In Connecticut, the new arrivals took up residence
in Kensington, part of the small town of Berlin immediately to the south of New Britain, before moving
later to New Britain itself, a city of over 40,000 and
one of the most vibrant industrial centers in the U.S.,
the home of Stanley Works; Landers, Frary & Clark;
Corbin; Fafnir; and other factories dating back to the
nineteenth century that made most of the country's
best hardware. The factory owners' mansard-roofed
mansions, the robust employment opportunities, and
the busy downtown suggested a city with a glowing
future. Josepha found work taking care of an elderly
woman of means during the day in Hartford (leaving when the woman's husband became rather too
friendly) and then a seamstress in New Britain. She
mastered English with a speed that surprised everyone, including herself. She made friends quickly, but
that wasn't surprising.

Josepha was on her own for over three years
before she was married in 1917, a few weeks before her
twenty-third birthday. It was a union that had more to
do with stability and expectations than romance, the
result of too many people she knew suggesting, subtly
or otherwise, that it was time to settle down and find
a man with a steady job. It was time to begin a family. Alois Schreiner, a master tailor, had been born

in St. Martin near Salzburg and lived for a time in Graz. He was thirteen years Josepha's senior, a fellow Catholic and German speaker whose English, even after sixty years in his new homeland, never became more than rudimentary. Their wedding photo is a study in stiffness even by the standards of the day, two people assuming a role for the camera that neither can quite bring off. Her wedding clothes do nothing to make the seated, veiled bride look more attractive, less stocky, less caught in something about which she has grave reservations; Alois stands tall, or as tall as a man of five-feet-six-inches can seem, his hairline already fast receding, his moustache clipped, his shoulders thrust back, standing over his prize with his hand on her shoulder.

The marriage was a mistake, and it was the last time Josepha would be talked into anything. It was a union that lasted nonetheless for fifty-two years, until Alois's death in 1973 at the age of ninety-two, and produced three children: Sigfried Alois in 1918, Virginia in 1920, and Marion in 1930. That son— known from childhood as Siggy—was stationed at Nichols Air Field near Manila at the time of Pearl Harbor and was to be a victim of the barbarity of the Bataan Death March and, for over three years, torturous conditions as a prisoner and slave laborer for the Japanese.

Considering Siggy's involvement in the U.S. war effort when he was in his early twenties and sub-sequent suffering as an American prisoner of war, it's worth noting that the position of his family in their adopted country, like that of most Austrian-Americans and German-Americans, was a precarious one at the time of his birth. Once President Wilson asked Congress in the spring of 1917 to declare war on the Central Powers of Germany and Austria-Hungary, anyone's familial ties to countries now deemed "the enemy" were suspect. The favored term in the local paper, the *New Britain Herald*, to describe the Allies' adversaries was the widely used, derisive epithet— the doughboys were crossing the Atlantic to fight *the Hun*—and when former president Theodore Roosevelt gave a rabble-rousing, xenophobic speech in Hartford in the fall of 1917, he warned the state's patriotic residents to be alert to "the enemy within"—namely, their neighbors from Germany and Austria who still retained any affection for (or, worse, even the vaguest loyalty toward) the country of their birth.

This was a time for immigrants from central Europe to be careful about what they said, the language they spoke in public, the food they ate, the letters they received from abroad. (And Josepha, writing in German, did make an effort to keep in touch with her family by mail.) As his English improved, slightly, Siggy's father joined thirty-one other New Britain men of Austrian descent in applying for American citizenship in 1918, the year Siggy was born. For male companionship, he joined the St. Stephen's Club and the Austrian Donau Club, two of the town's several ethnic fraternal societies.

In the 1920s and 1930s, Siggy grew up in the fashion of any number of other American boys of his time, class, and background: attending school a few blocks from his house, playing with friends in the town's many parks (the grandest of which was designed by the creator of New York's Central Park, Frederick Olmsted), perfecting his English better than his father had been able to, looking for odd jobs for pocket money. Playing hooky in high school, a problem Josepha soon rectified, for a time at least. I want the teacher who is making fun of him stopped, she told Louis Slade, the middle-aged principal in the pince-nez. I want him to finish high school. What Josepha wanted did not always come to pass, though.

There were also the Sunday mornings spent with the family—not necessarily with excessive enthusiasm on Siggy's part—attending Mass at St. Peter's Church on Franklin Square, the parish that catered primarily to New Britain's German, Austrian, and French Catholics, where Father Reywinkel's word was law and Josepha found a community of like-minded Austrian women. The weekend afternoons and evenings learning to drive. Learning to fix things, to become mechanically adept. Going to dances and movies at the Strand and the Palace. Looking for girls. Always looking for girls.

During Prohibition, like many Austrians, Alois made his own wine—of dubious quality—in the darkened basement of the house at 88 Ellis Street, which both Siggy and Virginia tried when no one was home. During the Depression, Josepha took in more sewing to supplement her husband's salary as a tailor and grew vegetables in their backyard. Almost miraculously, they were able to hang on to their two-story house with its ample yard, pear tree, and flower garden during the worst of the economic downturn, largely because of the upstairs rental income. Siggy grew up with a circle of friends of various national-ities as the neighborhood was full of German, Irish, and Scandinavian working-class families. Athletics mattered to him. He became a strong swimmer and a remarkably able gymnast, competing in state compe-titions, his physical prowess an unexpected source of pride to his parents. He was short (like his father, five-feet-six-inches tall), wiry, tough-muscled, and agile, attributes that would prove crucial for what lay ahead. There were ways, however, in which people of Siggy's background were once again suspect.

Indeed, there was even more reason in the late 1930s for Americans to look askance at their German- and Austrian-born neighbors than there had been at the time of World War I. Acquaintances of Josepha and Alois in the New Britain area attended the infa-mous pro-Nazi Bund rallies in New York and, on a trip to Germany in the late 1930s, the cousins she had emigrated with, who were at the time living on the second floor of the Schreiner house, had themselves photographed raising their arms in the Nazi salute. Josepha didn't share their anti-Semitic sentiments. The family she had worked for in Hartford was Jewish

and she found them appealingly cultured and intel-
lectual. She detested the fact that Joseph Rogan spoke
admiringly—all his days, practically—of Adolf Hitler.

It can't be said, though, that Siggy's decision to
enlist in 1939, even before FDR's peacetime draft went
into effect in the fall of 1940, was based on patriotic
fervor or a desire to show the world that Austrian-
Americans were as committed to Western democratic
values as anyone else. He hadn't finished high school
and, impressed as he was with his father's dazzling
skills as a tailor ("he could make anyone look good, he
took away all your flaws," Siggy said with pride), he
didn't last long working with him in the basement at
the high-end Art Jones men's clothing store on Main
Street near City Hall. The idea of service in the U.S.
Army Air Corps, and the possibility of being posted
overseas, sounded thrillingly adventurous. He was
a young man out for adventure. New Britain offered
few prospects in that realm. Siggy shared his mother's
willingness to take a risk just as she had done when
spending a year alone in Milan and beginning a new
life far from Europe. He went to the enlistment office
with two friends from town, Billy Swensk and Jack
Campbell, a buddy who had just finished a year in the
Civilian Conservation Corps. After his basic training
in New Rochelle in New York and a brief posting in
Michigan, Siggy was sent overseas as a private with
the Seventeenth Fighter Squadron.

By 1941, Siggy and Jack were both on duty at two
air bases—Siggy at the Nichols Air Field, Jack at the

Clark—in the Philippines, a U.S. possession since the Spanish-American War of 1898. A 1934 Act of Congress had promised the Filipinos their independence as a sovereign nation in 1946.

To be an American living in or near Manila in the early 1940s wasn't a burdensome proposition. On the contrary: for many officers who had a choice, it was a desirable posting. The capital of the Philippines was a relatively prosperous city of over half a million, equivalent to the size of San Francisco, its boulevards packed with two-wheeled horse-drawn carriages, Model T's, and the most up-to-date expensive cars and lined with bursts of hydrangea. American dollars went far. Officers could afford personal servants, often more than one, and had access to the city's polo fields and best golf courses.

For the enlisted men, the exchange rate was a godsend, too. For a dime, anyone could get a shave at his favorite barbershop. Five dollars was enough to have a pair of shoes expertly handmade by local Chinese shoemakers. The department stores were not very different from those at home, plentifully stocked with Western products. Cabarets and movie houses provided entertainment and weren't off-limits to any American in uniform on leave from the base. Liquor was easy to come by. The food was good at the local restaurants, though most of the men seemed to feel that what they could get at the camp's Mess was almost as good. Catholic De La Salle College offered popular film programs open to the public, which

the Americans took full advantage of. Some servicemen were sufficiently thrift-minded to open savings
accounts with Manila's Philippine Trust Company.
(For them, the weekend of December 7th, 1941, would
be the last they would see of whatever money they had
in those bank accounts.) General Douglas MacArthur,
his wife, and their four-year-old son lived in a suite in
the majestic Manila Hotel.

On leave in the city, American servicemen were
instructed to have a condom on their person at all
times—MP's regularly stopped servicemen on the
street and demanded to see that each man was following that order—should they feel the need to visit one
of Manila's many brothels, though the film instruction
about sexually transmitted diseases was as explicit
and intentionally off-putting as the Army could make
it. The Army didn't expect its young men to remain
celibate, but they did expect they'd take precautions. (One reason General Jonathan Wainwright,
MacArthur's second-in-command, was more popular
with the men than the more stiff-necked MacArthur
was that he could joke about the topic. At a staff meeting with its share of disheartening news, Wainwright
remarked that no month should be considered a
washout with only a single case of VD reported in
four weeks.)

Siggy's communications home before the war
suggested he was actually having the time of his life.
The workday for officers and servicemen began at 7:00
but pretty much ended with the searing heat of noon

time. (The regimen was less laid-back by the middle of 1941 when Japan moved its troops farther south into Indochina and rumors of a coming war were rife; the wives and children of officers, excepting MacArthur's, were ordered home that summer.) Siggy's duties at the air base repairing planes, Army vehicles, and equipment genuinely interested him. He had a talent for making friends quickly and he wasn't the kind given to homesickness. The camaraderie and roughhousing of barracks life suited his temperament. It wasn't anything like school back home. He was free from his father's discipline and his mother's expectations, and it was interesting to meet men from very different parts of the country. Despite the torturous humidity and soaking monsoon rains, he liked the outdoors

On the beach in the Philippines shortly before Pearl Harbor.

and physical activity of any kind, games played under the trees, pastimes—cards, horseshoes, jumping rope, slugging contests (where carefully matched combatants just aimed for their opponent's arms and shoulders), displaying his unusual gymnastic skills.

One photograph he sent back to New Britain was of a lithe, nicely tanned young man in a bathing suit relaxing on a tranquil beach, spelling out Christmas and New Year's greetings in the wet sand. It was a far cry from the cold winters of New England, he told his parents. He would always be a man for the beach, the sun, the warmth. The city on Manila Bay: it was a kind of paradise for a Westerner.

All of that changed on December 7th and 8th, 1941.

—∞—

Sigfried Schreiner's journal, upon which this account of his experience of the war years is based, evolved in fits and starts and under radically changing circumstances and began more as a diary than a journal. After the Japanese attack on the Philippines, the small notebook Siggy had purchased in the fall of 1941 was something he tried to write in almost every day, even if only a few lines, until the strain of combat and the deteriorating conditions on the peninsula of Bataan where the American troops had been sent, made keeping a record of contemporary events and impressions impractical and dangerous. "When Bataan capitulated [in April 1942], I had no choice but to destroy the original diary," he wrote later. There wouldn't be any place to hide it if the men were strip-searched by their Japanese captors, which ultimately proved to be the case. He had to recreate it later, in captivity again, for a time, but under less prying circumstances.

Then, after completing the seventy-mile forced march north to his first place of detention in northern Luzon, he began a second diary on scraps of paper picked up in different places, most of which he stole from supplies in a nearby Manila port terminal building. He kept it hidden in his pants for the better part of two years as he was transported from the Philippines to Korea and finally to China. At some point in 1944, though, he realized that his luck couldn't last indefinitely. Random Japanese "shake down" inspections too often led to the confiscation of any suspicious-looking papers and a beating with rifle butts by guards that left a man bloodied and barely able to stand. He needed to burn the diary or hide it in a more secure place.

Siggy approached a friend from Connecticut, Nick Bosko, who worked in the prison camp kitchen and secured from him an empty five-gallon soybean can. Two other buddies adept at metal-working helped him construct a regulation-sized canteen out of the larger can with a false bottom in it, the upper portion to hold water, the lower to harbor the diary. For the last fourteen months of his captivity, from June of 1944 to August of 1945, Siggy found it impossible to write anything, and that portion of his journal is based on his memories during his recuperation back in the United States in a Florida veterans' hospital in 1946. The pages, numbering over 300, that he asked his sister Virginia to type up for him in 1947 were a combination of salvaged scraps of paper and recollections composed from his hospital bed.

There was no question in Sigfried Schreiner's mind when he began his journal that what was happening in that first week of December in 1941 was going to be worth remembering.

He was right, of course. On Monday the 8th, he and the men in his barracks were awakened in the middle of the night. (The exact time varies among different accounts. Siggy remembered it as four a.m.) They grumbled about being dragged from bed for a drill alert at that hour, which had happened before more than once. They quickly learned that it wasn't a drill. A sergeant came in to announce the news of the attack on Pearl Harbor. That "stopped the grumbling—like a smack in the face," he wrote. Not even twenty-four hours after the devastation inflicted on the American fleet in Hawaii (only twelve hours, in fact, given the time-zone difference), the first Japanese aerial bombardments of the Philippines began. Any idea of American invincibility in the world disappeared overnight.

The kitchen staff slapped together a quick breakfast, but many of the men, Siggy among them, were too keyed-up to eat. Their first order was to head to the

supply room and arm themselves with the rifles and
pistols stored there, grab a gas mask and a shovel, and
retrieve any other equipment that looked valuable.
Their second order was to start digging foxholes like
mad at a distance from the barracks, buildings which
would be too easy a target when the enemy's planes
reached the air field. They'd be sleeping outside for
a very long time. No bedding, no cover overhead, no
mosquito nets. At nine a.m. the air warning system
gave notice that Japanese planes were approaching
Luzon, the principal island of the Philippine archipelago that included Manila, the Clark and Nichols air
fields and, on the other side of Manila Bay, the peninsula of Bataan.

It wasn't Nichols Air Field, several miles south of
Manila, that received the truly significant hit, though.
It was the Clark, over forty miles north of the capital, and that attack proved to be disastrous for the
Americans. Inexplicably, despite knowing what had
happened in Hawaii, MacArthur hadn't given the
order to keep every plane at Clark Air Field airborne
or moved south to Mindanao and out of harm's way.
Rather, many of them back from recent reconnais-
sance missions were lined up "like sitting ducks," as
one Japanese fight pilot later remarked in amazement.
Seventeen of the nineteen B-17 bombers on the ground
were destroyed with a fair number of the pursuit
planes also blown apart or damaged. Fifty-three P-40s
at Clark and nearby smaller airfields were finished
off. One hundred American pilots and soldiers on

the ground were killed and more than twice that number wounded.

Siggy wouldn't have known for some time, but his friend from New Britain, Jack Campbell, training to be a pilot, was among the dead in the attack on Clark Air Field that day, the first Connecticut man to die in action. He had graduated high school with Siggy's sister, Virginia. His body was never recovered.

It would only be a matter of another day or two, everyone knew, before Nichols was similarly ravaged from the air, and the next forty-eight hours before the anticipated attack finally took place on December 10th were spent dragging heavy kitchen equipment and supplies out of the kitchen, barracks, and offices into the bushes of the surrounding area and digging more and deeper foxholes. Men who had been in the hospital who weren't entirely healed were hurriedly discharged back into active duty to make room for the more seriously wounded that were starting to come in. One man Siggy knew still had a right hand that was all but useless, the result of a car crash two months before, and another had had his appendix taken out only a week earlier. In the context of an unprecedented emergency, they were judged well enough to be sent back to active duty.

The raid that came on the 10th lasted only forty-five minutes, but it seemed like hours to the men on the ground. No one had slept well with the constant buzzing of mosquitoes and the anxiety that never let up. "Nights were getting rough," Siggy noted. In the morning, he and his best friend, "Baron" Balukevich, were sent around inspecting gun pits until 11:45 when a truck pulled up with some food and the two men got in line with everyone else waiting to be fed. Just then "we heard the drones of motors and it made us uneasy," he wrote. Suddenly, there came "a formation of 35 Jap fighter planes from the direction of Fort McKinley, which was east of Nichols Field. We dropped everything." The men made a dash for the ditch that had been dug parallel to the runway. They landed on their bellies. The impact of the bombs raised the prone men right off the ground. Planes on the air strip were straffed. Aim was taken at a gas truck very near that ditch where Siggy and Baron were crouching; they were saved by the open fire of American planes returning from a mission against the Japanese in northern Luzon. One enemy plane, about to take aim at the control tower, was hit by an American P-40—"one short blast and the plane disintegrated in the air...[in] a cloud of smoke."

The loss of lives and planes was considerably less than what it had been at the Clark Air Field, but climbing out the ditches and foxholes, the sight that awaited the men was nightmarish. Crater holes dotted the ruined runaways. "All the barracks were in shambles, some blazing. An oil truck burned furiously at one end of the field....The P.X., tailor shop, shoe shop, gymnasium and hangars [were] shattered." Siggy and several of the men went into what was left of the supply room and the day room and salvaged some underwear, blankets, and canteens. They looked into the mess hall—can goods had been shot up by the bullets fired through the roof and food was splattered all over the room—and then grabbed fire extinguishers to help put out some of the smaller blazes. That night some of the men got stinking drunk on the beer they'd been able to find still intact in the refrigerator in the P.X.

Reports came in the next day of the complete destruction of the Cavite Naval Base on the south shore of the bay, thirty miles from Manila, and that disturbing news brought home the realization that there wasn't any large-scale landing site left in the entire Philippines for supplies or reinforcements sent by sea, should help ever be coming their way.

—∽∿∿—

Interestingly, Siggy doesn't seem to have been traumatized by the events of that first week of war. Waldo—"Baron"—Balukevich, his buddy from Nashua, New Hampshire, and the guy he most liked to pal around with, was similarly unflappable. For the moment.

Almost two years older than Siggy and a star athlete at his high school—a swimmer, a boxer, a track and football and baseball star—Baron was tall, muscular, and physically imposing in a way that Siggy wasn't, but the two were a perfect match. They took every opportunity during the lulls of the next few days—mainly while waiting for parts that never came to replace the equipment that had been damaged—to request leave to hitch a ride into Manila, even though the city had been subjected to scattered air attacks already. They knew that two Catholic boys in uniform

Siggy *(right)* and Baron Balukevich (c. 1941).

would find a warm welcome from the Christian Brothers at the De La Salle College in the suburbs of the city. They had a hot bath there. They wandered past the makeshift prison pen next to the college where the first Japanese prisoners of war, presumably downed pilot crews, were housed. They went out for ice cream bars and stayed at the college overnight to see the movie of the week, *The Last of the Bengal Lancers* with Gary Cooper and Dorothy Lamour—an odd choice for the school's film society to be screening, given that it deals with the British of the Raj at war with the natives during the Indian Mutiny of 1856, with scenes of Victoria's soldiers being tortured—but any movie was better than none, presumably. Who went a week without seeing a movie in 1941?

Two days later they were in downtown Manila, this time to see the comic *Buck Privates* starring Abbott and Costello as hapless enlisted men, at least as peculiar a movie for any cinema to screen under the circumstances, one would think. Some part of the aura of peacetime life, though, especially the comfort of a darkened movie theater, was hard to shed, even as things grew more unsettled on the streets of the city and nervous residents looked to the men in uniform as the defenders they were going to need. "Manila was wide open to the soldiers," Siggy recalled. "We could have anything we wanted free." He made an attempt to wire his parents, letting them know that he was alive and in one piece, but the government and the military had taken over all available lines.

The Schreiners had no idea of their son's fate at that moment.

Back at the air field, the next several days assumed an exhausting monotony. The routine was much the same: "Work like hell. Air raid at noon and fighting the mosquitoes at night." Until December 24th.

Baron and Siggy had been given leave to go back to De La Salle College that morning. They arrived at noon, luxuriated in another bath in the dorm rooms, talked with some of the teachers and students they knew there, and made their way toward downtown. But three short hours later, they were back at Nichols. Orders had come through that everyone was to report to their respective outfits. The night before, MacArthur had declared that, as of the 26th, Manila would be an "open city." He made that declaration in the hope—entirely misplaced—that it might be spared massive civilian casualties as the Japanese troops moved closer to the capital, and it meant that all Americans, military and civilian, had to leave. The full-scale invasion by the Japanese from the north was underway. MacArthur, his family, and staff left for the more secure island of Corregidor near the mouth of Manila Bay.

After daily, intensifying air raids across the Philippines, Japanese troops had landed in force on Luzon to begin what military planners in Tokyo had assumed would be a quick defeat of the American and Filipino forces as the Emperor's unstoppable army, navy, and air force made their way south to Australia.

By January, the Japanese understood that victory in the Philippines was ultimately going to be theirs, but it wasn't going to be as quick as they had imagined, and their own casualties were already considerable. The Americans were digging in and would fight to hold them back for as long as possible.

Christmas Eve at Nichols was hectic. The men packed their personal equipment, firearms, tools, and all the spare parts they could lay their hands on. "Engineers were detailed to destroy all the remaining equipment and the two runways that night. At four p.m.," Siggy wrote, "we saw the remaining P-40's come into Nichols Field to refuel for the last time." The men moved to the docks as the sun was setting. Transport boats were arriving to move them across the bay to the Bataan peninsula as soon as the engineers finished their demolition work later in the evening. With the flames of the last gasoline storage sheds rising high in the sky behind them, the boats started to take off at nine o'clock—at an agonizing crawl, as they had to navigate their way in the dark past mine fields and the hulls of American vessels that had been sunk during earlier air attacks. Siggy gave in to his overwhelming fatigue, "so exhausted I just laid down and went to sleep where I was [stretched out on the deck]. I faintly remember some men stepping on and tripping over me."

The War Department's plan in the event of an invasion of the Philippines had always been to consolidate American and Filipino forces on Bataan.

They were doing so now, but without the air and naval backup they had lost in the three weeks since the beginning of the war. Doing without an ongoing supply chain and any hope of massive reinforcements, or the availability of ships to evacuate the men to Australia if need be, hadn't been part of the original plan. The whole thing suddenly had the air of a precipitous retreat—into a questionable corner, no less. It was a "tactical withdrawal" that took days to complete and ultimately involved over 100,000 under-supplied human beings—80,000 members of the American and Filipino military (more Filipinos than Americans) and over 20,000 nervous civilian refugees from Manila and the surrounding areas who followed them.

When Siggy woke on Christmas morning, he and his outfit were at the Mariveles harbor on the southern tip of the peninsula. Hot cups of coffee were handed out as they disembarked. Their first order was to head north to Pilar to complete some reconstruction work on the airfield there. They didn't get very far before they were forced back for a time by Japanese air attacks on the road they were walking. Siggy made a rush for the nearest cover, which turned out to be a sewage ditch. While crouched there, he felt a burning sensation through the back of his pants. A tiny fragment of hot metal from an exploded bomb had hit him in the buttocks.

The work they had to do on the runways was quickly completed, but his journal isn't clear how long he remained there, though it would seem he was back on the southern edge of the peninsula at some point soon after as his supply sergeant was able to make the quick boat trip to Corregidor two days later to bring his outfit some fresh clothes, especially shoes as what they were wearing were fast falling apart. The menu for Christmas dinner at Pilar was clear in any event: canned blueberries, crackers, and ham. References to food in the journal are always exact.

Siggy's home for the next three-and-a-half months was a land mass twenty-five to thirty miles north-to-south and no more than twenty miles east-to-west, with an enormously varied terrain: mountain ranges stretching down the center of the peninsula, flat open plains, miles of rice paddies and sugar cane fields, steep ravines, thick jungles, thick banyan trees, dirt trails, crisscrossing streams, sandy beach shores lined with cliffs. The dense vegetation at least provided good cover when Japanese planes soared overhead. Two roads, one paved and one of cobblestone, ran for miles but neither covered the entire north-south expanse of Bataan. The most significant problems: thick vines that formed sometimes near-impenetrable barriers, water that was not always potable, and reports of pythons, more disturbing even than the ravenous malaria-spreading mosquitoes and the ubiquitous flies, spiders, and leeches the men now had to live with.

The Filipino troops who were moved to Bataan with the Americans were at all times able, praiseworthy fighters, Siggy noted, though some sized up their grim situation early on and, disappearing into the jungle after ditching their uniforms, sought to blend in with the natives who lived inland in small villages. No one blamed them.

The American men lived on rumors—none of which, sadly, turned out to be true. They'd all be in Australia in a few weeks. Australia was sending planes to replace the downed American aircraft. A rescue convoy from Hawaii was on the way. The enemy would never be able to make it all the way south to take the whole of Bataan, given the terrain and American resolve. MacArthur could be counted on to have a plan.

—ᴡᴡ—

At the same time, a growing sense of chaos, of control slipping away, was pervasive. On December 28th, Siggy recorded watching a dog fight in the air above him, the men cheering on a much-liked pilot, Lieutenant Elmer Powell, as he took down two Japanese planes before circling over Manila Bay to come in for a landing. The over-excited Filipino soldiers manning the gun batteries proceeded to shoot him down by mistake. "When he reached the shore, he and we were so mad we could have killed all the Filipinos. He was lucky to have escaped uninjured. We were infuriated because planes were precious and couldn't be replaced." The same thing happened to *two* U.S. planes the next day. Siggy was willing to acknowledge that, while the shooting down of Lieutenant Powell's plane was inexcusable as P-40's did not look like Japanese planes, the P-35's could be mistaken in the heat of the moment for enemy aircraft. Nonetheless, headquarters detailed extra personnel to serve as plane-identifiers at all anti-aircraft positions.

Not that the Americans didn't make their own missteps. One night, a private named Hale was on guard duty. A staff sergeant, Holtman, got up to relieve his bowels. "Hale heard some rustling in the brush, hollered once, then opened up with his rifle hitting S/Sgt. Holtman in the arm. The medical man Brown dressed the wound and the following morning he was evacuated to the hospital. From that time on, everyone took extra precautions in letting the man on guard know when they were going out in the brush." Another man, a staff sergeant Siggy knew from his basic training days in Michigan, shot a hole in his hand while cleaning his 45, though a few of his comrades wondered if the injury was truly an accident. Seriously injured men were being ferried to Corregidor to be looked after by medical teams there before eventually being sent to Australia.

For their part, Siggy and Baron did their best to keep their heads down, follow orders, and appreciate the fact that they were in an area that was doing better than others in the supply chain. "Baron and I had the detail of stacking all the food supplies. We arranged them in such a manner so we could sleep on them at night. We stretched a tarpaulin over it to shelter us and the food supplies from the rain." The rain was beginning to be a problem.

A bigger, more catastrophic problem was evident to everyone by the middle of January. Siggy and his friend were on the food distribution detail. "At this point we were feeding two meals a day. Breakfast at 5:00 a.m., if you could call it such, and the other meal at 4:00 p.m. This consisted of one or one-and-a-half sandwiches per meal with a half canteen of coffee." Energy levels dropped significantly at that level of sustenance.

Did this have to be? The fact that once hostilities began in early December (and the U.S. war plan had always involved a mass movement to Bataan if Japan invaded), the most essential supplies—principally food rations—hadn't been transported immediately across the bay by the Army Quartermaster from the ample food storage areas in and around Manila and from the well-stocked Army food dispensary to the north in Luzon—that lapse mystified and angered the men. It was an egregious error on the part of MacArthur and his staff not to have made that need a first priority. One problem was that MacArthur has always been convinced that the war wouldn't start before the spring of 1942.

Within days on some parts of the peninsula, within weeks on others, but by late January everywhere, the amount that came in by the relay of trucks—the dozens of loaves of bread, the cans of salmon, the thirty pounds of rice meant to feed an entire squadron and an increasing number of civilian Filipino refugees—diminished until, finally, there wasn't any bread at all coming through or enough fish and rice to go around. Half-rations had been introduced early in the month. Soon Siggy was reporting that his daily food intake was half a peanut butter sandwich and a mess kit-sized helping of rice pudding. The period of slow starvation began.

The men at that point had no choice but to look out for themselves. The mules and horses were dispatched first. Boys from Montana, Idaho, Wyoming, and the western states who knew how to skin and roast *carabaos*, the Philippine water buffalo usually found wallowing in mud, were put to work doing that; at least it was meat and the *carabaos* were easy targets to bring down. Plants were dug out of the jungle soil, but that involved more guesswork than expertise as to what was edible. Attempts to catch fish in the bay went on non-stop whenever there weren't any enemy planes in sight and the area was thought to be clear of snipers. The tails of the lizards they caught—and the lizards, really iguanas, were everywhere—were actually pretty good, Siggy thought, something close in taste to roast chicken. There was a drawback. He couldn't help recalling "how I have seen them feasting on the bloated bodies of dead Japs."

Then there were the monkey hunts. The scrawny tree-climbers were shot, skinned, and cooked by hungry, increasingly desperate men. (Once skinned, the monkeys "resembled an infant about three weeks old," Siggy wrote, which made cutting them up and forcing yourself to swallow what you'd just cooked an ordeal.) Not surprisingly, on this kind of diet, painful digestive problems, maddening rashes, and edema of the feet became a problem as beriberi, caused by a shortage of the vitamins the body needs, took its toll.

Another issue, a shocking failure on the part of the U.S. military planners, was the age and inferior quality of the firearms and ammunition, and the frequently useless hand grenades, with which the men were provided. How was anyone to deal with the advancing Japanese forces and the small raiding parties they sent ashore on all sides of the peninsula with such abysmal equipment? Every man was, in effect, an infantryman now, every man would be a front-line fighter sooner or later, but the machine gun Siggy was issued kept jamming after two rounds. He was later given a rifle that looked as if it had seen duty in the previous war. Grenades would be thrown if the men heard, or thought they heard, an enemy sniper in the brush, but they sometimes didn't explode. A sinking feeling set in across the lines in January: were they being abandoned in an area that their superiors knew—but no one of rank wanted to say aloud—was being written off as certain to fall to the enemy, no matter what?

Anger toward MacArthur among many of the men turned to rage. While he and his family and staff,

who had also left Manila on Christmas Eve, were relatively safe in a tunnel complex on the nearby island
of Corregidor, the men on the peninsula were slowly
descending into a hell of starvation and despair.
Despite the need to bolster morale among his anxious
troops, which all of his subordinates remarked on to
him, their commander made the crossing to Bataan—
three miles away, five minutes by torpedo boat—only
once in the seventy-seven days he was on Corregidor,
and that was in early January.

The general and his retinue toured by car some of
the defenses and field hospitals and spoke the predict-
able encouraging words. They were disturbed by the
worsening conditions the men on Bataan were living
under, though MacArthur's reports to the president
of the Philippines and the U.S. War Department
told a different story, making groundless optimistic
predictions. Everywhere, though, the toll of malnutrition and dysentery was beginning to be apparent.
MacArthur promised the men he met that help was
on the way, though he must have known, or certainly
strongly suspected, by that time that such wasn't the
case. "Dugout Doug" became the common, fiercely
derisive term for their commander among many of the
American servicemen.

Four days after that one and only visit to Bataan,
MacArthur issued a statement to be read at every
encampment. "Help is on the way from the United
States," it read. "Thousands of troops and hundreds of
planes are being dispatched. The exact time of arrival

of the reinforcements is unknown as they will have to fight their way through the Japanese attempts against them. It is imperative that our troops hold until these reinforcements arrive." Not a word of it was true.

Another problem was that sometimes—too often—the Japanese soldiers who were caught and were supposed to be brought north to Baguio to the American interrogation center that had been set up didn't arrive there. Their Filipino guards, incensed at the invasion of their country, simply shot them on the way. "We questioned the scouts," Siggy wrote, "and their only answer was 'But, Joe, they tried to escape.'" From then on, Americans were sent to bring the prisoners to Baguio.

Not that an inordinate number of prisoners were taken. The Americans soon learned that Japanese propaganda officers had told their soldiers that if they were captured, they would be tortured and that they'd be outcasts never free to return to Japan, the humiliation to them and their families would be so great. They were expected never to be taken alive. They were also expected never to retreat. As a result: "The boys now had plenty of trophies, including rifles, pistols, sabers, flags, money, etc." The packs of cigarettes Siggy had accumulated, he gave away as he didn't smoke. Yet. He would later.

Not having been trained for the infantry or to handle any significant artillery, Siggy was part of a group that had disparate non-combatant duties: principally, food collection and distribution from areas where supplies, meager as they were getting to be, were still available, but also, for hours at a time, digging machine gun pits, stringing barbed wire across pathways, and making hand grenades out of bamboo filled with dynamite and fuses, which in his view were more dependable than the ones issues by the Army. It was draining work. Whenever everything was finally set up in a given area to an officer's satisfaction, the crew was moved on to a different location. The general in charge of the peninsula, Edward—"Ned"—King, came by to make an inspection one day and pronounced himself pleased with the machine-gun pits Siggy and the members of that team had dug.

So much time in a truck on the road, though, meant that Siggy and his fellows were more apt to be the target of a bombing. At the end of January, he wrote, "We got our orders to move to kilometer 191 [near Agaloma Point on the western shore of the peninsula]. Before we moved out, a Filipino artillery unit took over our positions. It seems like every time we complete a position and get everything in order, we would have to move again." On this particular day, the 28th, the enemy's bombers seemed to be all over, the roads constantly being dive bombed. "This road was very zig-zagged and a Jap bomber was trying to get us lined up. We expected it at any minute, but it seemed as if God was with us." God wasn't with the better target ahead that the pilots spotted and suddenly veered away to attack. When Siggy's truck arrived at the scene, they saw the wreckage, American soldiers' blasted bodies strewn all over the road and hillside.

By early February, more and more men on the front lines were starting to contract malaria, so Siggy served as a replacement for several days that month. He emerged unscathed but saw more than he wanted to. "Our first casualty was Lt. Frank Brezina. He was killed by a Jap booby trap. It consisted of a hand grenade wired up so that it blew off his face as he stepped over a fallen tree....Corp. Barnhart was also wounded by sniper fire. He was shot in the center of the back and Capt. Bronk, the squadron doctor, removed the bullet with a half hour using a very limited supply of equipment." Absent any mention in the journal is whether Siggy killed any Japanese soldiers himself.

That same day, the Americans had some luck when Japanese planes dropped supplies to their own men who were encircled in the area, but a number of the cannisters that were parachuted down landed within American lines. "Chocolate bars," Siggy exulted. "Hershey's, no less. Lucky Strike cigarettes. Ammunition. We kept the food and cigarettes. The rest we sent to headquarters."

There were advantages to moving about so often. Coming upon a clean pool or stream of water, the men could strip, bathe, and wash the only clothes they had with them now, which stank and were full of lice. They could ask about friends they hadn't seen since leaving Nichols Field and could trade gripes about officers. They could also gather the news that other outfits had picked up on the radio. None of it was encouraging. They heard that the Russians were falling back before the Nazi onslaught and that Singapore and Rangoon had been taken by the Japanese. Not a word of any relief headed their way.

Fellow feeling made a difference. Knowing that someone had your back, or at least wasn't oblivious or insensitive to the condition of the men around him, meant something. That wasn't happening, in Siggy's view, across ranks by February. Bluntly put: "The officers were beginning to get indifferent to the men. [Three lieutenants] were hi-grading the food supplies, leaving the scraps for us." There were a number of volatile arguments and accusations over this breach of protocol, but they did little good. Who could they complain to in the chain of command? In the increasingly disorganized, even surreal world of the jungle, the old sense of military order and respect for command seemed to mean less and less. "There were also three Filipino girls in the [officers'] camp area. They girls slept in a tent near the officers. These girls were included in our rations and the officers made them wash their clothing and help them out in various ways. [It's impossible to tell if the wording at the end of that sentence refers to sexual favors or not. It seems a reasonable suspicion.] The enlisted men were not allowed in any part of the area around the officers' and the girls' tents." One of these girls was kind enough to help out "Ski," another friend of Siggy's, who came down with malaria before he was taken to a field hospital. Malaria—the sweating, the wasting, the mental fog, the difficulty walking—was now everyone's worst fear.

—⟋⟍—

The decision to surrender on Bataan was made in early April by Ned King. Four months of crippling bombardment, attacks from Japanese snipers, firefights on the shore and in the jungle, and the slow but inexorable movement southward of the main body of the Japanese infantry—coupled with the now extremely dire food shortages and the illness of many of the men—had led to an untenable situation for the Americans. MacArthur, his family, and staff had already departed Corregidor for Australia a few weeks earlier after a certain amount of pretense on MacArthur's part that he would stand and die with his men. General Jonathan Wainwright was left in charge.

The surrender was a complicated, acrimonious business, though. MacArthur didn't believe in surrender under any circumstances, but he wasn't there anymore to direct events. Wainwright didn't want King to surrender, either, but ultimately knew the decision had to be his, and King was convinced that further resistance would simply mean the deaths of the thousands of American soldiers and the tens of thousands of Filipino soldiers still hanging on, for all of whom he was responsible. In continuing to fight, they might take just as many thousands of Japanese

soldiers with them—MacArthur's preference—
but they would beyond a certainty be killed to the
last man.

The Japanese command initially thought that
General King was surrendering all American forces in
the Philippines and were furious when he explained
to them that the men of Bataan would be laying down
their arms at his order, but that he had no authority
to speak for the smaller forces on Corregidor. Only
General Wainwright could do that. General Masaharu
Homma was angry and incredulous. The result of that
furious argument was that, while the men of Bataan
had put down their arms and were being herded north
to detention centers, the fighting continued against
Corregidor for another month until Wainwright
(again to the displeasure of MacArthur in Australia)

Major General Edward King discusses terms of surrender
with Japanese officers.

saw the futility of further action. The complete surrender of all American forces in the Philippines didn't take place, then, for another month. General Wainwright declined to leave and, along with many of his staff, was taken prisoner as well.

The aura of invincibility belonged entirely to the Japanese now. Guam, Wake Island, and Hong Kong had fallen within days of Pearl Harbor, Singapore in February, the Dutch East Indies in March. The complete takeover of Burma, invaded in December, wasn't completed until April, but its fate was a foregone conclusion. The archipelago of thousands of islands that constituted the Philippines was now to be incorporated as well into the Empire of the Rising Sun or, as the Japanese preferred to term it, the Greater East Asia Co-Prosperity Sphere. Like Admiral Dewey's U.S. fleet attacking the Spanish in these same waters forty-four years earlier, Japanese ships sailed effortlessly into Manila Bay.

Their abject defeat didn't come as a surprise to the Americans. On April 9th, 1942, Siggy had noted, "I went to sleep last night downhearted." The day before everyone had heard that the Japanese had decisively penetrated the American lines throughout Bataan and that every man, no matter what his previous assignment was, might be called up for combat duty again. There was no point in worrying about food distribution, more machine-gun pits, or stringing more barbed wire. "It was then that I realized that we had really lost."

During the night enemy planes bombed Mariveles Field. "The bombs sounded like ash cans coming down" Siggy wrote. "The concussion knocked me from the hammock I had strung up between two trees. At four a.m. we heard more explosions. At first, we thought it was shells from Jap artillery but then we realized it was our men destroying the meager supplies that remained at Little Baguio. At dawn our platoon commander, Lt. McCullen, had received the order from General King that we were to surrender at noon that day."

The first order of business at daybreak was to destroy every piece of usable equipment. "The 50-caliber machine guns and ammunition were thrown into the bay," Siggy remembered. "Rifles and pistols were smashed on the rocks." He threw his camera in the bay, buried his diary. Everyone who had Japanese currency taken from prisoners or the bodies of the enemy—or those with some sense of what was coming—buried that as well. Men caught with yen later paid dearly for having that souvenir found on them. The men ate everything left in the supply area, mainly coconut meats, and finished disarming.

"I threw my rifle in a gully after smashing it on the rocks," Siggy wrote. "Then Baron and I packed our bags with necessary supplies and started for kilometer post 180 [as they had been directed to]. As we walked single file down the trail with the leader carrying a white flag, the Jap observation planes were circling overhead keeping a watchful eye on

everything." Their captors were waiting for them at
different points along the way to organize them into
manageable numbers.

After assembling at the Mariveles Air Field,
the men were searched willy-nilly and stripped of
anything of value or utility—food, watches, pens,
rings, razors, sunglasses, knives and forks and
spoons (though some were left with their American
or Philippine currency)—and then lined up to be
marched north in what promised to be searing heat.
Some were allowed to keep their canteens; others had
them grabbed and thrown into the bushes. Some were
viciously pushed to the ground, kicked in the shins, or
slapped in the face; others left alone. Some men were
searched more vigorously than others. There seemed
to be a randomness to everything, a lack of any system, as they started out. This first encounter with the
Japanese had more an air of wildness, of frenzy. This
was plausible: there were too many prisoners, too few
guards in proportion to the staggering numbers of the
surrendered, and too many enemy soldiers worked
into a white rage by the deaths of their own friends
and the hard fight the Americans had put up.

Siggy took a risk by hiding his watch in the tightly
rolled-up sleeves of his coverall and his money inside
his canteen cover. He took another risk, when the men
were given a break to sit in a field for an hour in the
scorching sun, by sneaking off to a stream in a nearby
gully and splashing water on his face, plunging his
bare feet into the cold stream, and filling his canteen.

He stayed close by Baron. It was painful to spot "Ski," a friend who still should have been resting in a hospital bed, trudging along in a daze, and they were later able to get him a place on a truck for the those who were truly unable to walk "and that was the last we saw of him," Siggy wrote, "for some time."

They were going to walk, they were told by the few interpreters in their midst, to San Fernando, seventy miles north, though their ultimate destination would be Camp O'Donnell, an uncompleted U.S. induction center near the destroyed Clark Field that would now be used as a prison camp. It was a walk that took those who had been at the southernmost point on the peninsula five days to complete without provisions being made for food or water. It was open country, meaning "no shade, plenty of dust and heat; also plenty of dead bodies of Americans and Filipinos in the roadside as this was where we had made our last stand." They slept that first night on the ground in a downpour.

—∞—

Word of the capture of the Americans by the Japanese was received at home by everyone, but especially by families like the Schreiners, as the realization of their deepest fears as spring approached in 1942. The press in Connecticut and elsewhere labored to find something—anything—encouraging to say. Consolidating his forces on the peninsula has been "a bold and skillful maneuver" on the part of General MacArthur,

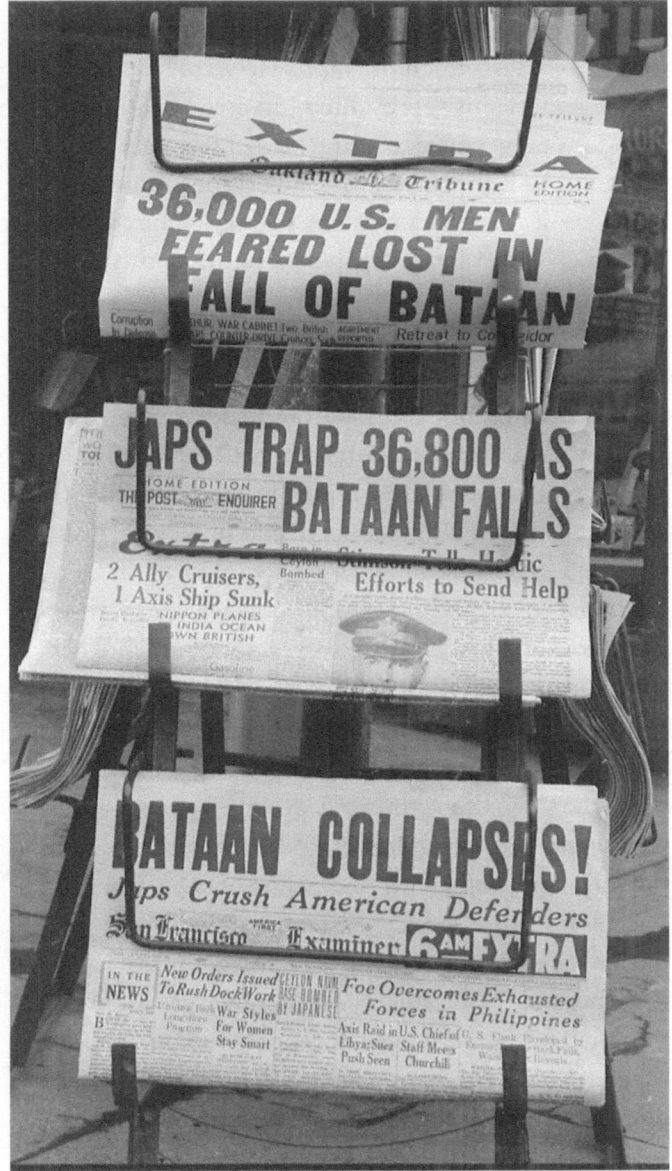

Newspapers

the *Hartford Daily Courant* maintained, and the four long months in which the Japanese were held back by the Americans represented "an epic of gallantry, of indomitable courage in the face of tremendous odds...[to be remembered as one of] the greatest episodes of America's military history." The Sunday editorial writers lauded a "heroic fight" against impossible odds.

The families of the men taken prisoner might have looked at a headline in that same statewide paper that week as more expressive of the horror they felt: "Enemy Tidal Wave Engulfs Bataan." A New Britain family read a speculative report in the paper that their son, Louis Rio, a high-school friend of Siggy's, was assumed to be among those killed. (He was, in fact, alive and survived the war.) If Louis was dead, Josepha and Alois had just cause to worry about the fate of their son.

Yet no one on the home front could imagine what was about to take place on the Bataan peninsula any more than the thousands of U.S. servicemen could who were about to endure it. Indeed, it wasn't until the following year, with the escape of some imprisoned servicemen from their captors, the Davao Dozen, as they were called, that any details of the treatment of the prisoners while they were force-marched out of Bataan were reported to General MacArthur in Brisbane and the War Department and the White House. The men were instructed to say nothing publicly for several months, for that matter, and it wasn't until 1944 before the American public finally learned—for those who could stomach them—the details.

The sadism of the captors of the American and Filipino soldiers on their march north was a disorienting, destabilizing experience for everyone. The possibility of dying in combat, of being blown to pieces by a bomb dropped from the air or being shot, hadn't been far from anyone's mind after Pearl Harbor and had changed everything about life in the Pacific. But what the Americans on Bataan encountered from the moment of their surrender and the beginning of that march was completely unexpected. Whether raised back home in big cities or suburbs, small towns or farms, whether they watched the newsreels at local theaters or not, no one was prepared for the complete disregard for the rules of war and the passion for degradation their captors showed.

Anyone who knew the details of the Rape of Nanking in 1937, when Japanese violence against Chinese civilians had shocked even the Nazi diplomats in that city, might not have been surprised, but very few Americans had an intimate knowledge of what had transpired—the beheadings, the burials alive, mass rape, the obscene photographic recordings they made of their own abuses—when the Japanese invaded China five years earlier. They were learning now about the darkest side of human nature and that Americans were not immune from its effects.

It wasn't long before the atrocities started. "Two brothers behind me were in tough shape," Siggy wrote. "One had malaria and the other was trying to keep him going, but they lagged behind, and finally the Jap guard separated them, making the one that was physically fit go on and the other fell to the ground where the Jap guard bayoneted him while his brother looked on." A Filipino boy who looked as if he couldn't have been more than eighteen made a mad dash for the brush. "The guard spotted him and in a few seconds we heard the report of his rifle. Apparently, he missed shooting the boy, but we knew he had killed him as he came out from behind the bushes wiping the blood from his bayonet." The men who were wobbling and sweating the most—men who looked as if they might soon suffer a fatal heat stroke—had their hats grabbed from their heads and thrown aside. This was known as the "sun treatment."

Everyone who walked too slowly, who collapsed by the side of the road, or stopped to help someone who did, was liable to feel the crack of a rifle butt on his head or the blade of the bayonet in his chest or back. The same was true for the men who broke out of the lines when they saw a stream nearby or a chance to escape. There were too few guards to catch everyone who did. Seeing a sugar cane field close by, several men did just that. Siggy took another chance and made a break for the field with them to grab some of the sugar cane he could yank from the ground and devour quickly. He saw others filling their canteens in the ditches beside the field. Several feet away, the bloated bodies of men and horses filled that same watery ditch.

Passing the stiffened cadavers of so many dead Japanese in uniform along the way told the defenders of Bataan how dearly the Japanese had paid for their victory. But every time a Japanese guard looked at an unburied countryman, the blowflies and maggots feasting on that body, he was apt to take his anger out all the more aggressively on the men in line. Worse for everybody was the smell, which was inescapable. The smell of decomposition, the smell of vomit, the smell of excrement.

When the part of the line Siggy was in reached the outskirts of the town of Balanga on the eastern side of the peninsula, more than halfway to their destination, they were herded into a large field and told they would stay there until morning. It wasn't a restful site: "[It] reeked from the odors of decomposed bodies that were laying there for days. This didn't bother the men at all. Some would sit down beside the bodies and eat their meager supply of sugar cane, while others would lie down and go to sleep. Baron and I dug up some raw turnips we found in the field. With this, [and] with some rice we salvaged from a stream where the Japs had thrown it, we made a meal. Some men had diarrhea which didn't help matters any, and it was hard to find a place to sit or lie down."

He recorded witnessing an instance of suicide. The next morning the prisoners passed through some small villages and a few Filipino soldiers ran out of line to get water. A guard who saw them clubbed them frantically to the ground, and the ones who weren't able to get up as quickly as the guards wanted were bayoneted and thrown into a ditch beside the road and left to decompose. Shortly after that, the line of men approached a bridge over a dry riverbed. An American officer—he looked to Siggy to be about fifty and he wasn't able to determine his rank—cried out loudly, "I can't stand this anymore." He jumped. He died instantly. It wasn't the last suicide Siggy would witness.

The Filipino residents of the villages they passed through on Luzon were moved by this gruesome spectacle, both for the soldiers of their own country and for the Americans. As endless lines of exhausted, skeletal figures passed by them, they sometimes threw sugar cakes, bananas, or rice wrapped in palm leaves to the emaciated men. The guards slapped the men, women, and even the children who were doing this. When the Japanese at the front of the line told the villagers they encountered ahead not to aid the prisoners in any way or they'd be shot, they still gave the men the "V for Victory" sign when the guards were looking elsewhere.

Siggy seems not to have witnessed two of the most horrific actions of the march, the beheadings by a quick thrust of a saber that ended some American soldiers' lives—along with the trauma of those buddies near them having to see this—and the forced burying alive by Americans of men who were near death but hadn't yet expired. Other memoirs attest to those atrocities. By the time the captives reached San Fernando, though, no one had any illusions about what their future treatment would be like. When they first surrendered, a few American officers had tried to be encouraging and talked to the men about the Geneva Convention and what it said about proper treatment of prisoners of war. Wasted words. The Geneva Convention, which those officers didn't seem to know Japan had signed but never ratified, meant nothing to the men holding the rifles, the bayonets, the sabers, barking orders in a language their prisoners didn't understand. No one knows how many Americans died over those five or six days, but the estimate is several hundred. Many more were on the verge of death when the march ended, and over the next few months the number climbed well into the thousands, but as many as several thousand Filipinos died in that one week in April, 1942.

There was also a hideous practical aspect to the rampant killings which the Americans and Filipinos couldn't have known about. The Japanese had been truly stunned by the size of the surrendering armies, native and American. They were expecting to have to corral, minimally feed, and guard something in the realm of 50,000 men. They were completely unprepared for having to deal with well over 70,000 captives. Their officers wanted those numbers culled before the Americans and Filipinos left the peninsula.

From San Fernando, where there was a railway line, the men were loaded at four in the morning into box cars to be transported to the town of Tarlic and from there to Camp O'Donnell. The thirty-two mile trip to Tarlic took six excruciating hours. The cars were of a size to accommodate forty men, Siggy guessed, but a hundred were forced in. Men fainted from the heat and the lack of air. At the town of Capas, they were let out for two hours and told to line up. Not for relief or out of pity. It was two hours of the "sun treatment." Then, after arriving in Tarlic, the walk to Camp O'Donnell began, seven miles away.

Arriving at the camp, the men were lined up, some barely able to stand, in front of the main building. They were searched again—some for the fourth or fifth or sixth time since their surrender—and made to listen to a speech, more like a fanatical rant, from the camp commander. The United States should know it could not win against the Japanese empire, he screamed at them. It was foolish of them to think they could. The Japanese could, and would, wage war against the West for a hundred years if necessary.

Siggy and Baron entered the building they were directed to. They confronted a demoralizing situation: "As there was no room to sleep [there], Baron and I had to sleep under [the building]. The food and water situation was critical. We got two meals a day consisting of watery rice called 'lugao.' Water was especially hard to get as the pump which supplied the necessary water usually broke down three or four times a day.

There seemed to be endless lines of men waiting for water. It was impossible to wash [but] you were happy enough to get water to drink...The latrines were nothing but a trench dug in the ground swarming with maggots which helped to increase the number of flies in the area, spreading disease."

A week later, Siggy and Baron were moved, and the area they were originally placed in was turned over to the medics to be used as the hospital for the camp, though not to much purpose as "the doctors didn't have any medical supplies to help the men sick with dysentery and malaria, so they just laid there until they died." The water by then was coming from a dirty stream about a mile away, and everyone was instructed to boil it before drinking. Many of the Filipinos were so dehydrated they didn't wait to do that. "In a few days they started dying like flies."

The dead, both American and Filipino, were buried in an area three feet deep and fifteen feet square. "The bodies were thrown into these graves in a haphazard manner and covered up." One problem was that it became hard to tell the silent but still-living men from those who were actually dead, their pallor and weight was the same. The bodies were placed under the building, "but there were some living men put there by mistake." In one instance, Siggy and Baron pulled out one body they were instructed to bury. They left it for a few minutes to do something else and when they returned it was gone. It was back where they had first moved it. They reached under and felt for a pulse: none was detectable. "Again we removed the body from the beneath the building and this time watched it. Sure enough, a few minutes later he came to life and crawled beneath the building again."

Some of the men had the luck to be assigned to work details outside the camp, and they occasionally returned with extra food, on occasion with the all-important quinine needed to ward off malaria. Bartering these precious goods—for cigarettes or cash—became commonplace. At this point, it was evident that personal initiative might make the difference between survival and ending up in one of those shallow graves. Baron and Siggy understood that their guards in their part of the camp wanted someone to wash their dishes and mess kits. They managed to get themselves picked for that detail, which came with the tacit understanding that they could eat any leftovers in their guards' mess kits.

A group to be sent outside the camp that included Siggy and his friend was organized at the end of the month, the purpose of which wasn't made clear to them at first. They were later told they would be put to work salvaging the equipment that was still in the hills throughout Bataan—i.e., firearms, ammunition, search lights, telephone equipment, car parts, trucks that could still be driven—and bringing it to a central depot so that it could be processed as scrap metal and sent to Japan. So it was back to San Fernando and then points south, one hundred of the men to Balanga and the other hundred to Bagac. Siggy and his friend were with the latter group at first.

At San Fernando, they noticed that the bodies they had propped up in a schoolyard were still there. As the truck Siggy was in started on its way out of town, one of the men stood up to get a view of the scene. "As he did so," Siggy wrote, "an overhead wire caught him by the neck and jerked him from the moving vehicle. He hit his head on the concrete pavement and was killed instantly." The Americans tried to persuade their guards to let them bury him, but they weren't stopping for that. He was left on the road.

Arriving at their destination, the men were given a mess kit of rice and some dried fish, and the next day Siggy's contingent proceeded over rough roads to Bagac, where they began work the following day. That was when Siggy's first attack of serious diarrhea started and his every rushed trip into the bushes infuriated the guards. Luck was with him, though. After his recovery, one of the guards, a man named Yukio Hikita, spoke English. He told him he was a teacher before the war. He asked Siggy if he wanted to be his "cook man." By that he meant a servant in every way: building fires, cooking, washing the mess kits of Hikita and four of his friends, scrubbing and drying their clothes, being at their beck and call. Siggy leapt at the chance, knowing that it might an opportunity when no one was paying attention to grab some extra food—more rice, more salted dry fish (but less moldly than what was given to the prisoners), a few greens, and, especially appreciated, the vitamin pills they had. He was able at odd moments to sneak some food into his pockets for his friends. He soaped and rinsed his own clothes with those of his captors, who probably knew what he was doing, and was eventually allowed to have two other Americans to help him with his tasks.

That extra help didn't last long. The two men developed dysentery and were sent back to Camp O'Donnell fast. The guards were desperately afraid of catching something from the Americans, Siggy had observed. His own health, once he was no longer having to run to the bushes, stood him in good stead at the moment. A food dump had been discovered in the hills, which included jam, flour, spaghetti, and other canned edibles. Siggy was allowed some of the find. He also had the chance to bathe once in a while; the men he worked for didn't want their personal servant too dirty or germ-ridden.

Some Japanese soldiers had found a fifty-gallon gas drum in the brush, which they cleaned, cut the top out of, and set on top of a pile of rocks. The drum was then filled with water and heated by a fire underneath, and once the fire was extinguished, the Japanese would take a warm bath, with the highest-ranking officer getting in first to soak "and so it went on down to the lowest-ranking man." Once in a while Siggy was given permission to use the makeshift tub after everyone else. He was also given a mosquito net by one of his captors. They last thing they wanted was the malaria that was beginning to overtake more of their prisoners to spread to their side of the encampment.

Siggy soon learned to his dismay that Baron had come down with malaria and was being sent back to Camp O'Donnell as were all the Americans who were too ill to work. "I gave him the extra food I could steal," he wrote, "but what he needs in quinine," and that precious liquid was something Baron's friend had no access to.

The summer brought showers, and the threadbare canvas of the tents offered no real protection from those driving rains. In the fierce wind storms that accompanied the rains, the tents often collapsed, anyway. He and a new friend from Pennsylvania, Joe Stanko, found a car in the area. It had been stripped of its motor and wheels, but it provided a better place to sleep.

Tempers frayed, regularly, even among the Americans. One officer in particular seemed to live in his own fantasy world, Siggy and the other enlisted men felt, forgetting where they were and how little his own rank mattered now. A guard told Siggy to take some rice out of a bucket the officer had and bring it to him. "The major said if I took any rice out of that particular bucket, he would have me court-martialed when we got back to the states. I told him, the Jap has a gun so I'll obey him. So I guess he's going to court-martial me. What a laugh. He's the one who should be court-martialed."

By late July, the salvaging work was considered done, or as complete as it was ever going to be, and the men were told they would be going to a new camp that had replaced O'Donnell as the principal detention center. Their captors had their own qualms about this end of the metal-salvaging mission themselves. Some of them were afraid to the point of openly weeping in their anxiety that they were going to be sent now from the safer Philippines to more active combat areas.

Strangely enough, a tentative element of bonding had taken place between some of the guards and their prisoners. One of them gave Siggy, Stanko, and a third friend a letter in Japanese. "He said if we ever got into trouble with any Japanese soldiers to show it to them and it would help the situation." Two other Japanese soldiers, Little Sato and Ollie (the Americans had made up names for the guards they interacted with most regularly) brought a few Americans with them to a house of prostitution in Balanga. They were told to wait in the yard while they were busy with the girls they had selected. Outside "the girls gave the men some money and food while the Japs were being entertained," which was probably the expectation all along of the Japanese who brought them there. Then Little Sato, wanting a break from work, stole a truck one day to go joy-riding and invited an American to go with him. A bad driver, he smacked the vehicle into an abutment of a bridge. No one was surprised. When reporting the incident, he naturally blamed it on the American, which his commanding officer surely knew was a lie, and the officer "slapped Little Sato around for disobeying orders."

A couple of worrisome days followed as Joe Stanko came down with a bad case of malaria and was delirious for the better part of forty-eight hours until some quinine was found for him, and Siggy had a few bad spells of diarrhea, the pain from which was so bad that he thought it was an attack of appendicitis. A medic assured him it was the food, not his appendix, that was laying him low. En route to Cabanatuan, the new camp, their captors let the men out of the trucks to buy fruit, rice cakes, and candy from the townspeople in the barrios they passed through. When the convoy wasn't stopping in a town, the Filipinos would just line the road and throw candy and fruit into the truck's baskets, which the Japanese found amusing and made no effort to stop.

Heading to this new prison camp, past the barbed wire and the armed patrols, Siggy's fervent hope was that he would get word about Baron and another pal, Joe Mariello, who had been taken there. He did. They were still alive. The new arrivals met hundreds of Americans from Corregidor who told them in detail about the fall of the Rock, as it was called, Wainwright's capture, and the particular hell they had gone through (information about which Siggy devoted more than a dozen pages of the part of his journal written after his liberation).

If the men had hoped conditions at Cabanatuan would be at least marginally better than those they had experienced at the horrendous Camp O'Donnell, they learned soon enough that was not the case. The food was meager and atrocious, they slept on beds made of hard bamboo, and one of the guards used a golf club on the backs of the men he felt weren't moving quick enough in their assigned work detail. Malaria and dysentery, the usual illnesses, were rampant; medical treatment, almost non-existent. The area designated as "the hospital" seemed to Siggy to be constantly filled with an uncountable number of men. "Zero Ward" was the part of the hospital where the men who were certain to die within the next twenty-four hours were left. When cases of quinine arrived, sent by the Philippine Red Cross, the guards liked to hold it back for a few days, tauntingly saying that it had to be "inventoried." One night one of the men suffering from dysentery was in such a weakened condition that he fell into the latrine trench which was filled to the top with watery excrement. No one heard him fall in. He drowned.

Siggy was put on the dreaded burial detail for the several weeks he was in Cabanatuan, an assignment which was both backbreakingly arduous and macabre. (The one advantage for the men digging the graves and doing the burying was that they were given a much-needed extra bit of food, namely, a bun a day.) "At first [the graves] were made large enough for twenty men," he recalled. "Later on, we decreased the size to a ten-man hole. At times, the rain would make the ground muddy and hard to handle. Also, some of the bodies we had previously buried started to rise out of their graves, and now and then an arm or leg would be exposed above the ground. At times, the holes we dug would fill with water before we had a chance to bury the bodies and they would be floating around until we had to push them down with a stick or our foot and hold them there until they were covered up." The bodies by then were scarcely recognizable as people—"nothing but skin and bones"—and the rain formed a green scum around the graves.

The stench, not surprisingly, was "unbearable." Those men on the detail who couldn't stop retching had to be replaced. Eventually, the number of the dead became so great that the small building serving as a morgue reached capacity and bodies had to be left lying outside. Rumor had it that anyone with gold fillings in his mouth had them removed before the body was taken away. Every one of the deceased was stripped of all his clothing and buried naked as every item of clothing was needed by the living. It was impossible to preserve even a shred of dignity for their fellow men-in-arms who had passed away. Some on the burial detail covered their comrades' genitals with clumps of grass; that was the best anyone could do.

Punishments for infractions were draconian. If anyone escaped, the other nine men in his squad would be summarily executed. One man from the 200th Coast Artillery, a Mexican by birth, managed to get away and, passing himself off as a Filipino, got a job in town. The men at the camp heard about this and got word to him of the impending executions. He gave himself up. First, he was beaten by the guards, then shackled—loosely enough so as to be able to walk but never to run away again—put on permanent latrine duty, and forced to wear a placard around his neck advertising his transgression. Two other men made their way outside the compound and their buddies were about to executed, but the bodies of the two were soon found not far away. "Both apparently had been delirious [with malaria] when they died," Siggy wrote.

On another occasion, five enlisted men were taken by the guards who had caught them communicating through the barbed wire fence with local Filipino men. Their only offense, they insisted, was trying to talk the locals into securing more food for them. The officers who interrogated them refused to take that as the fact of the matter, wanting to know if they were attempting to learn more about the progress of the war from those civilians outside the camp or if they were trying to talk the Filipinos into fighting back against their invaders. The five Americans and two Filipinos caught by the Japanese were tied to stakes just outside the camp and left there with no food or water for forty-eight hours. The mid-day heat was excruciating, and one of the men managed to loosen his bonds and run back into the camp for water before collapsing on his own bunk. The guards accused him of attempting to escape, even though he had obviously run back *inside* the camp. The five

Americans and two Filipinos were then lined up
and shot.

"The diet we received at Cabanatuan would not
sustain normal life": that became clear even to their
captors as the daily death toll mounted past any burial
detail's ability to deal with it. "The Japanese finally set
up a system by which we could buy some food, if we
had money, and provided the orders were placed well
in advance." There was some hope of improvement
when a new camp commander arrived. It turned out
to be Mori, "a little on the stout side, and with a bris-
tling black moustache"—now Lt. Colonel Mori of the
Japanese army, a man who used to run a bicycle shop
in Manila and was well-known to the men. He had a
convenient memory, however, and pretended not to
recognize any of his old customers, and so nothing
changed in terms of diet or punishments, though
the death rate did drop from thirty a day to twenty
between mid-summer and September. That drop,
Siggy assumed, wasn't thanks to Mori; it was simply
a matter of the weaker men having already breathed
their last.

A visit to the camp of an English-speaking
Japanese general in early September was carefully
scripted. The men were instructed to answer any of
his questions briefly and respectfully and otherwise
not to speak to this "great personage." One American
officer did point out how many men were too ill
to stand in the ranks for his arrival. The general
inquired why this was the case. "We are all starving,"

he was told. "'That will be enough,' said the Japanese general. 'Your men are not starving. They need more exercise.'"

Shortly before his departure from Cabanatuan, Siggy witnessed one of the worst tortures inflicted on men caught trying to escape, in this case two army officers and a naval civil engineer. They were beaten about their calves and feet until they couldn't stand and jumped on with their captors' full weight. The next morning, they were stripped of their clothing except for their boxer shorts, and with their hands tied behind them and in full view of the camp, pulled up by ropes that forced them to remain upright for two days, during one of which they were pelted with rain from a fierce storm. When the rain stopped, the Japanese corralled any Filipino men walking on the road near the camp to strike the men in the face with a club. "If the Japanese did not think the Filipinos put enough force into their blows, they themselves were beaten," Siggy wrote. Blood splattered the trees nearby. The men's faces were unrecognizable, "with the ear of one prisoner hanging down by his shoulder." Siggy concluded: "I think we all prayed for the men during this ordeal. I know I did. And I am sure all of us said a prayer of relief when the Japanese finally cut the men down and took them away for execution. Two of the men were shot. The third was beheaded."

—〰—

Prisoners were being dispersed by October, some reportedly to work in Japan and others to prison camps in Manchuria and elsewhere. They were first taken to Manila, packed into boxcars with no toilet facilities. At the Manila train station, members of the Filipino Red Cross were waiting with medicine and stretchers for the disabled. They weren't allowed near the Americans. The few glimpses the men had of the city they had once so enjoyed were discouraging. Manila, once a thriving metropolis, showed the effects of war and occupation already. "The people have a frightened look about them," Siggy wrote. There didn't seem to be a car on the streets, and the devastation caused by aerial bombardments was visible everywhere.

At the dock where they were to board ship over the next few days, the men were left on their own to find a place to sleep. Siggy found a space in the lavatory of a building which, without working plumbing, wasn't in use. Anyone who had to relieve himself had to do so right off the dock. The day before his departure, Siggy spoke to a guard who knew some English. "I bribed [him] to get me some tea from a restaurant nearby. "This he did for a nominal fee," he recalled, "which depleted my bankroll by five pesos."

On October 6th, 1942, Siggy and the men in his contingent were given a loaf of bread, which they were told had to last them two days. They were then herded—about a thousand men—into the hull of a freighter and told to stay put until the ship was well outside the harbor, at which point they'd be allowed to come up for air.

The name of the ship was the *Tottori Manu.* Its destination was unknown.

—⋙—

Back in Connecticut, Siggy's parents and two sisters lived from the time of those first devastating reports of the fall of the Philippines for fifteen months, until March of 1943, never knowing if their son and brother was even still alive. At the start of that second full year of the war, the government was finally able confirm that he wasn't listed among the dead but was most likely a prisoner of war. Having written more than twenty letters to their son in the weeks after Pearl Harbor, all returned unopened, Josepha and Alois were at least relieved to know that much. Virginia continued to write letters c/o the Red Cross. "I didn't know if he got them," she said years later and received only one terse, vague reply from him in return. Still, she kept writing, praying. (In fact, many the letters mailed from New Britain did get through eventually, but they were delivered sporadically. When the Soviet army liberated the prison camp in Manchuria where Siggy was being held in 1945, sacks stuffed with correspondence from family members in the U.S. were found dumped in the back of one of the offices. Once they were opened and distributed, Siggy discovered dozens of letters in those bags addressed to him.)

The stress at home during his absence was compounded by the awkward family dynamic that had only gotten worse during the summer and fall of 1942. Josepha and Alois only rarely got along—the age difference exacerbated tensions in a small house—and, as their daughters remembered it, they weren't able to find the means to comfort one another. Marion at twelve, clinging to her mother, had to make what sense she could of a grim situation while still trying to have some semblance of a normal childhood. Virginia at twenty-two, missing her brother but wanting to carry on with a social life of her own, seemed to provoke her mother's resentment much of the time.

As the months passed, a gloom that became more and more pervasive settled over the Schreiner home at 88 Ellis Street in New Britain a few blocks from downtown. Alois could barely bring himself to talk about his missing son. He spent more time at his club. Siggy's sisters missed the older brother who had doted on them, knew how to tell funny stories, had an irreverent streak, and stood up to his father's Old World sense of discipline. As a teenager, he once took the strap out of his father's hands that was about to be applied to him and chased Alois around the backyard with it. Marion had howled with delight.

Holidays were painful occasions now. Christmas of 1942, before word came from the government about Siggy's status, was scarcely acknowledged as Josepha fell into a deep depression. Marion spent that Christmas Eve lying on the living-room couch with her mother, her head in her mother's lap, as Josepha sobbed quietly and uncontrollably. Easter, Thanksgiving, and subsequent Christmas celebrations had their share of similar distressing moments.

Virginia's relationship to her mother, made worse by the obvious fact that she was her father's favorite, suffered as Josepha frequently took her anger and despair out on her eldest daughter. Virginia had been working as a typist in Hartford during the three years since her graduation from high school, was dating, and attempting to live the life of an attractive young woman in her early twenties. Father Reywinkel counseled Josepha to look to her faith for sustenance and refuse to give up hope. Siggy's mother was a devout Catholic, but that advice was more easily offered than embraced. Worse, the news from the Pacific suggested that the war would be over in Europe long before it was on the other side of the globe, where it most mattered to the Schreiners. The president had even confirmed in public at the start of the war that priority would be given to first toppling Hitler and liberating Europe.

It was a frustrating period. Families weren't sure how to assimilate the news from the war zone. Hope battled with a sinking sensation of despair. The release of the Hollywood film *Bataan* in Connecticut movie theaters in 1943, starring Robert Taylor, George Murphy, Lloyd Nolan, and Desi Arnaz, certainly didn't do anything to reassure the Schreiners. Everyone dies in the movie—fighting valiantly, of course—though the ending promises an eventual triumph and a retaking of the Philippines. All the family could do was hope that Siggy would be one of the lucky ones and that his survival instinct would see him through whatever he was enduring.

—〰—

Siggy's survival instinct was, in truth, very strong. That determination to make it through the war entailed two strategies, if one wants to call them that: not thinking too much about the future and shutting down emotionally to the nightmare he was living in then, a process that always exacts a toll later. Siggy was twenty-three years old, and how many hundreds of men had he seen die in unspeakable ways? How many thousands of bodies had he seen decaying, baked in the sun and scavenged by insects? How many

Bataan movie poster. (1943)

men had he been forced to bury in shallow graves? How could he deal with the uncertainty he felt about the fate of friends like Baron or the lack of any news about how the war was progressing? What effect does gradual starvation have on anyone's body and mind?

That self-protective "shutting down" was impossible during his time on the *Tottori Maru*, though. It was one of the vessels later designated as the "hell ships" by the Americans. As promised, the prisoners were allowed to come up to the deck for air and a last glimpse of the Philippines once they were on their way, but that was the last act of humane treatment the men were to know for their next few weeks on the water. The *Tottori Maru* was a floating prison meant to break the spirit of anyone who still imagined he could take whatever was meted out to him. In a dank space that could at best accommodate a few hundred men, three times that number were crowded together with minimal toilet facilities, two water tanks, and one meal of rice a day. They shared the space with some sizable rats who scampered about at night and with endless voracious lice. In such tight quarters, men lying down and too weak to get up urinated on each other, excrement covered the floor that the men without shoes had to walk through to get to the water tank or to claim their rice, and many of those who had boarded the ship in poor health to begin with succumbed and were thrown overboard with a piece of scrap iron tied to their feet. Siggy woke up one morning to discover that he had been sleeping all night next to a dead man. Seasickness affected almost everyone. The nausea never stopped. Periodically, the Japanese on deck would taunt the men below by throwing cigarettes into the cargo hold and watching them fight over them.

As the ship had no markings that would enable the American submarines in the area to differentiate it from any other Japanese vessel, it was subject to torpedo attacks. On the first day out, the *Tottori Maru* was almost hit, but the torpedoes passed on each side of the ship. With few life preservers and a limited number of life boats, which the Japanese would naturally have claimed for themselves, a direct hit, all the men knew, would have meant everyone below deck would have gone down with the ship. The lower holds were crammed with the scrap metal that had been retrieved from Bataan, weight which would have led to a quick descent to the bottom.

The men who were obviously about to die were carried off the *Tottori Maru* at their first stop, which was Takuo in Formosa. There the ship was disinfected in a perfunctory way and the men were told to strip naked on the dock, in full view of passing Japanese women and children amused by the sight, where two fire hydrants were opened to hose them down. Modesty wasn't an issue. The water felt good.

The ship continued on to Pusan in Korea, by which time the men were finding the conditions they were living under unendurable. The lines for the latrine had become so long, it could take hours before one could get in. Men started using empty biscuit boxes to defecate into and, when they were full, threw the contents over the side when they were allowed up on deck. "A couple of times I thought I was going to die," Siggy wrote. "The lines were too long for me to wait so I just went over the side of the ship. First I would vomit and then turn around to defecate. This went on till my stomach was so sore I could hardly move." Angry and despairing moments were inevitable. Patience was exhausted. A Navy man, a veteran of twenty-five years, used a razor blade hidden in his pants to slash his wrists. One American beat another American serviceman to death when he caught him stealing from him. *Steal everything you can lay your hands on from the Japanese* was an unwritten rule among the prisoners; steal anything from a fellow prisoner and no one would take pity on you.

A third of the prisoners, Siggy included, disembarked in Korea, the rest proceeding to Japan. The weather turned bitterly cold. Not everyone had shoes. The men were issued a fresh, lice-free pair of pants, a coat, a shirt, and an overcoat. Those who had survived the voyage were going to be put to work for the Empire now, and so a minimal degree of concern for their health was finally of some consequence. The need to further humiliate the men was a constant, though. They were paraded from the docks through the center of town to the railroad station, another opportunity, as Siggy put it, "to show the populace how the superior race had captured the degenerates."

The Americans were expecting to make the three-day trip to their new site of detention, Mukden in northern China, in something like the suffocating boxcars they had been transported in previously. Instead, they were put onboard a passenger train with assigned seats, four to a row, two each facing one another. It was a difficult sleeping arrangement, but far preferable to the experience of the boxcars. They were instructed to remain in their seats at all times except when they needed the bathroom, never to talk to, or motion toward, any Chinese people they saw when the train pulled into a station, and not to throw any food their way through an open window—the last as stupid a directive as could be imagined. What were they thinking, Siggy wondered. "We eat all we can lay our hands on," he wrote. The Americans weren't about to give any away to strangers.

The food they were given (rice, salmon, pickled beets, tea) was an improvement over what they had been forced to consume on the Bataan march or at Camp O'Donnell or Camp Cabanatuan—again, an indication that their captors wanted them in reasonable shape to work when they arrived at their destination in Manchuria. At one stop, they picked up another carload of prisoners, British and Australian servicemen and officers who had been captured with the fall of Singapore. They were soon to meet some Dutch and New Zealand captives as well.

—〰—

Siggy's train arrived in Mukden (Shenyang today) on Armistice Day, November 11th. The camp was three miles northwest of the city. "It was very down-heartening for us as it was cold and dismal." They disembarked from the train and were trucked to the camp. Formed in columns again, the 1,300 men heard the usual harangue from a Japanese colonel about the greatness of the Japanese Empire, had their first glimpse of their new home ("a sea of mud"), and were sent to their assigned barracks. They were given numbers to wear at all times over their left breast pocket. The numbers from 1 to 100 were set aside for officers, but there weren't 100 officers among them, so the officers' orderlies were given those numbers as well. The enlisted men's numbers then ranged from 101 to just over 1,500.

Siggy was now Number 124. He wondered if he would die in China in an unmarked grave and be known solely by that dehumanizing designation. New Britain, home, St. Peter's Church, and the Catholic cemetery where his family expected to be interred seemed immeasurably far away.

The barracks were constructed of wood and built partly underground. Walls were packed with dirt for insulation against the biting cold and the wind. Each building was divided into two main sections with two small rooms at each end that were equipped with a small stove made of brick. The larger section was heated by three larger stoves. He counted nineteen barracks in all.

To everyone's surprise, that first afternoon the men were issued four blankets a piece. That was their first indication of how frigid the winter nights were going be in Manchuria. Siggy and two other Connecticut men—Nick Bosko from Norwich (#125) and Teddy Olslager from Hartford (#126)—agreed to sleep huddled together under their pile of blankets. Very little of their efforts helped, though, as the building was constantly "damp and uncomfortable." The stoves didn't provide enough heat. Nor did sleeping fully dressed make much difference. It snowed on their second day in Mukden, the first snowfall Siggy had seen since leaving the United States.

Life quickly assumed a schedule—a rigid, unchanging schedule. Awake at 7:00 a.m., the men stood for *tenko* (roll call) at precisely 7:20 a.m. and then proceeded to the Mess at 8:00 a.m. for a breakfast of two small brown rolls (which Siggy judged to be "a little stale but edible") and a small cup of pork and barley soup. The other two meals of the day didn't vary much from the breakfast fare. At the evening *tenko*, everyone had to be properly attired, every button buttoned, and seated on the ground (no matter how cold it was) in a neat line with their feet tucked under their buttocks and hands on their knees. One man caught whispering to the fellow next to him during *tenko* was slapped across the face repeatedly by a Japanese guard. As a number of the guards knew

English, anyone who felt an urgent need to communicate something to a fellow prisoner needed to be especially careful what he was whispering about.

The camp commander explained to the men that first morning that they were there on a thirty-day trial, and if they proved to be obedient and showed sufficient strength and willingness to labor as they were told to, they would be allowed to write home and to receive a weekly issue of cigarettes. The principal work most of them would be sent to do was in the Mitsubishi factory in the city making machine parts, where they'd be given a small salary. They would be allowed to recover from their previous ordeal before being sent to the factory and were expected to sign a pledge, which the men thought completely ludicrous, not to attempt to escape. "I don't believe the signing of this pledge will stop any of us if we had half the chance," Siggy observed. What was clear, of course, was that they wouldn't ever have half a chance, and that fleeing into the vastness of Manchuria wouldn't solve anything. Where would they go? Two hundred miles north to Siberia? Several hundred miles west to Mongolia?

Siggy wasted no time in getting assigned to kitchen duty. Nick Bosko had already been sent to work there and he offered to bring Siggy and Teddy in with him. Teddy refused, but Siggy knew from working as a "cook man" on Bataan that any proximity to food supplies was a good, possibly life-saving thing. The kitchen proved to be a pretty disorganized place

("too many bosses"), with some of the men showing up
to get what they could while doing the bare minimum
of work. They were quickly replaced, but Siggy appreciated the initiative of the two men he worked under,
the resourceful Arnold Bocksel, a warrant officer from
Long Island, and Andy Pruvusnak, an army sergeant.
They talked the Japanese into letting them build an
oven in the water gallery so they could bake their own
buns every day for the men instead of making use of
the three-day supply of buns that was being trucked
in from the city twice a week, which meant the bread
was going stale by the third day. The construction of
the stove was preceded by a long argument with the
commander about whether it should be built of brick
or stone, but anything the kitchen staff could do to
make life more bearable for the men was worth the
effort, they felt. The few times when the right number
of supplies hadn't come through, the kitchen staff
went without and passed their share on to the particularly needy men in the barracks. And one time when
a Japanese officer came through to conduct one of the
many intrusive inspections of the facility, he declared,
based on no evidence, that too much food was being
wasted by the staff and cut their rations for one day to
make his point.

The ranking American officer at the camp, the
much-disliked Major Stanley Hankins, a notorious
alcoholic, could be just as annoying. He came into the
kitchen one day and complained that the help was getting too much to eat. Siggy was furious and indignant:

"He's a fine one to talk. When he and his fellow officers are having baked potatoes, meat, and special loaves of bread made, while the enlisted men in the barracks are eating stale buns and watery soup." He also conceded: "I don't blame Bocksel for giving the officers the extra food as he has to live with them and they can make it miserable for him." Major Hankins' rages extended to anyone caught taking food back to the barracks, even for a sick friend, and those fits of temper were not something anyone wanted to be on the wrong end of.

All knives and sharp instruments used in the kitchen had to be counted and brought to one of the guard posts every day. The reason: "The Japs were worried about us killing ourselves." Theirs had been a low, subtle transformation from a body of men their captors couldn't wait to see die, painfully, in massive numbers to a potential work force that would aid the war effort now that the Allies had recovered from Pearl Harbor and were fighting back hard. The American victory at Midway four months earlier and the Doolittle air attacks on Tokyo, which took place only days after the surrender of Bataan, had made the outcome of the Pacific conflict a little less certain now. The men at the Mukden camp knew nothing about Midway or the Doolittle raids, of course, and the Japanese wanted to keep it that way.

Siggy's duties consumed his day: hauling wood for fires, hauling coal, washing buckets, and cutting vegetables for hundreds of men. The vegetables were crucial as large numbers of men were now suffering from the opposite of dysentery: constipation that went on for days and weeks. He and his friends on the staff also had to listen to the British complaints that they didn't know how to cook anything properly, i.e., the way they were used to. The Brits petitioned the Japanese commander to start a mess hall of their own and were eventually given permission to do that.

Sometimes the camp diet allowed for slight variations, which was always appreciated—on random mornings sweetened maize was added to the breakfast menu—and as the weather grew colder that November, woolen underwear and heavier shirts were distributed. None of this helped those men who were truly sick, however. By the middle of the month, Siggy estimated that the death rate at the camp was one man a day, seven days a week, all buried on a hillside about a half mile from the camp. A bathhouse was set up for the use of the prisoners, who were told they could use it once a week. Bars of soap were sparingly distributed. The problem was no one wanted to use the bathhouse at all, no matter how dirty they'd become, because the building where the tubs were placed was too cold and most of the men were afraid of catching a cold that could lead to pneumonia, a result that everyone rightly believed was probably a death sentence. Once in a while, Siggy braved the cold to get clean. He regularly went to the fellow POW who had been assigned to be the camp barber to be shaved and have his hair cut as short as possible. Less hair, fewer lice.

The Japanese interest in keeping records of their prisoners seemed odd, but at least it implied, presumably, that they weren't all expected to perish at Mukden. For instance, every man had his photograph taken. Siggy noted that the pictures made everyone look "like hardened criminals. Some with heads shaved; others with beards, but I guess we all have the same desperate look upon our faces." They were also weighed. "I tip the scales at 112 pounds," he wrote—a loss of twenty-eight pounds since Bataan. The order to fill out "classification cards" which were intended to determine the kind of labor the men were best suited for provided the occasion for some fun. On the line asking the men to identify their occupations before the war, some wrote "Gambler," "Hitchhiker," "Tramp," "Jitterbug," and "a few more crazy titles." The Japanese in the office were initially confused by those cards and made the men redo them. The jokers were punished for their impertinence, but everyone in the barracks had a good laugh about it.

Concern about disease wiping out the entire camp was evidently on their captives' minds as well. Mitsubishi executives had made clear their need for workers with some degree of stamina. The men walked to and from the factory in town and were expected to be on their feet for eight- or ten-hour workdays. Workers who could barely stand were of no use to them. In the new year, the men had their urine and stool tested and were given typhoid and smallpox inoculations. There also seemed to be some interest in

reporting back to Tokyo the causes of so many deaths.
A team of doctors arrived purportedly to perform
autopsies for a week on some of the bodies before they
were buried. They have plenty of men to work on,
Siggy noted. The morgue where the autopsies were
being performed was roped off, but Siggy could see it
from the kitchen window. When they were done, the
bodies were thrown outside into a narrow wooden
coffin and nailed shut. The ground was too hard yet to
bury them.

A new camp commander, Colonel Genji Matsuda,
had arrived in December. The outgoing commander
left the men with an unexpected gift: 250 toothbrushes and some tooth powder, a much-appreciated
health aid of which Siggy was one of the recipients.
(The health of the twenty-five men who worked in
the kitchen was obviously a priority. They had to be
up at four a.m. to have breakfast ready for everyone
else at eight o'clock, then head back in the kitchen in
the afternoon to prepare lunch and later dinner, all of
which was accomplished with a frustrating turnover
in staff. Indeed, the necessity of rising in the dark on
the coldest winter mornings was the hardest part of
his job, Siggy felt. He was happy when he convinced
his friend Teddy Oslager to join the kitchen crew.) No
one expected gifts from Colonel Matsuda. One of his
first edicts was that, if he ever heard any complaints
about the food, the men's rations would be cut.

—∞—

An unheroic fact of life is that hunger and cold will bring out qualities in men that are more about need, anger, and desperation than camaraderie and altruism, and Siggy's diary records more than a few instances of belligerent behavior among his fellow prisoners. On several occasions, it was discovered that food intended for patients in the hospital wasn't making its way there from the kitchen. It was either being eaten by the kitchen staff or sold on the flourishing black market that existed in all camps. Stealing extra food from the kitchen wasn't in and of itself considered wrong—Siggy did it plenty of times—but taking it from the sick and dying, very wrong.

Even worse was the thievery. Over the course of one month that first winter in Mukden, Siggy's toothbrush, scarf, and a pair of socks went missing from his bunk when he was on duty in the kitchen. The wooden lids from the toilets from one barracks sometimes disappeared when someone wanted more firewood for his own freezing barracks. Fistfights over anything that rubbed someone the wrong way broke out in the barracks, though sometimes the men swinging punches were too weak to inflict any significant damage on their opponent.

On the other hand, there were moments of fellowship and vital social interactions. Fortunately, the men weren't stopped from visiting any of the other nineteen barracks before evening *tenko*. Siggy's pal Joe Stanko, whom he'd last seen at Cabanatuan, paid him a visit. "He looks like hell," Siggy wrote, but he was greatly relieved to know he had survived his time on the "hell ship." Men from the same state or region back home could share reminiscences. Playing cards made of scrap paper allowed for lively card games at night. One American who knew German gave Siggy and another man cursory lessons, as much a way to pass the time as anything else, though Siggy had some familiarity with the language from listening to his parents. As Christmas approached, the men practiced carols and planned their holiday meal. Their captors had agreed that they could have extra rations that day, but the meal had to include some kind of meat, everybody agreed. The reality of obtaining it was pretty clear: "The only meat available [that] is still living... happens to be the dogs from the nearby village."

Dogs tended to roam under the barbed-wire fence into the camp with some regularity. It took a few tries to "hit the jackpot," as Siggy phrased it, but the process of watching the dog die, who was big and didn't go quietly, was stomach-turning. Catching the animal in a noose when he went for a piece of bread left outside the barracks, "Butterball" (the self-appointed dog-catcher of the barracks) then drew the rope tight against the door so that the dog couldn't move and hit him over the head a good twenty times with a piece of iron grating. The animal was tied to a beam in the ceiling inside and skinned. "They made an awful mess of it as they did not have a sharp knife," Siggy observed. That night "'Butterball' and his clique had dog steak. "He invited me to taste some of it. It was not as bad as some people would think." Less gruesome in the capture but less filling was the sparrow meat another group shared.

On Christmas Day, Siggy had to work longer hours to keep the fires going for the extra food that was being prepared—soup with noodles, soybeans, pork slices, and carrots—and Butterball managed to trap a second dog. Arnold Bocksel, head of the kitchen detail, gave each man working under him a few cigarettes as a Christmas present, and another friend gave Siggy a pair of mittens. (That good-hearted friend, Robert Rosendahl, was one of the last of the Mukden survivors alive in 2020, dying just short of his ninety-ninth birthday.) Unfortunately, on the day after the holiday, Siggy developed a severe fever and wracking chills. He felt so depleted he wasn't able to go to work that day or the next. He was worried that this was the prelude to pneumonia, but felt better the following day after downing a "dog chop" ("It tastes somewhat like rabbit meat") and taking some quinine pills. A friend who worked in the hospital, Jack Lee, insisted on sneaking him in there for a blood test. It was malaria, but a mild case. The Japanese doctors didn't want to give him any more quinine pills, but the sergeant stole some for him, and by New Year's Day he was more or less back on his feet with intermittent recurrences over the next weeks of the sweating and the chills. When he was well enough, he started to boil his clothes. The lice had become an excruciating problem.

Early in his time at Mukden, Siggy took up smoking. It was allowed inside the barracks but not outside. When Siggy was found smoking outside at the end of the month, the guard on duty took his number and he waited for the summons to headquarters. The usual penalty was three days in solitary confinement in the guardhouse, sleeping on the floor with no blankets, no matter how cold it was. Sometimes the malefactor's hair was cut when he was released, usually in a bizarre, humiliating, tonsured fashion. The guard never did report Siggy, as it turned out. His friend Frank Gagliardi was caught doing the same thing and slapped by the guard who saw him.

So much was random in this hellish situation—who was punished, whose infraction was let slip by, who was slapped right and left because a guard just felt like slapping an American, who lived or died and who acquired one particular ailment or another. Nick Bosko developed two infected teeth. His face started to swell. The swelling became so severe that both his eyes were practically closed. He was excused from his kitchen duties and eventually taken to the camp hospital, but the infection was judged so bad that the teeth couldn't be extracted right away. An American medic working there managed to find some sulfa pills for him and he was brought to a hospital in the city so the teeth could be drilled to drain the puss that had accumulated and, finally, removed. One of Siggy's toenails became infected and had to be removed. That was a painful ordeal. More dire cases were those of the two men in Siggy's barracks who developed gangrene. One had his right leg amputated and another his big toe.

The camp was a rumor mill, naturally enough. Those who worked at the factory in Mukden and overheard their Chinese coworkers talking were the primary source of information. Some scuttlebutt was spot-on: the rumor for the day, Siggy wrote happily on March 26, 1943: "Germany is beginning to feel the pinch of the war." With the Allied fire bombing of Hamburg and the Soviets' ability after Stalingrad to curtail the Nazi drive into the USSR, that winter did represent a turning-point period for the previously unbeatable Third Reich. The news that Rommel was being pushed back in north Africa was true as well. Other rumors Siggy heard—that the Allies were landing in Spain or that the French had risen up against their Nazi occupiers and Vichy collaborators—were thin-air concoctions.

The rumors that most mattered to the men at the Mukden camp, obviously, were those that pertained to the war in the Pacific, and any hints that the U.S. Navy was retaking any of the islands conquered by the Japanese were especially welcome. Reliable news about that was much harder to come by.

—๛—

Did Siggy know at the time about the medical experiments that were being conducted at the camp on

American prisoners? It seems he did not, but there are
sentences here and there in his diary and the journal
that suggest he did perceive that something out of
the ordinary was happening. In February, the area
around the hospital was roped off and the men were
told that anyone approaching it would be severely
punished. Some men wondered about the appearance
of Japanese doctors out of nowhere. Was it plausible
they had arrived just to perform autopsies? They
wondered about men who disappeared from their
barracks for no known reason and weren't seen again
for weeks. Only after the war would most of the men
who spent three years in Mukden learn about what
had been done to their fellow prisoners by Japan's
biological warfare division. The victims had had
been injected with bacteria to study their immunity,
or lack of immunity, to various diseases. Those men
who survived these insidious procedures were often
extremely reluctant in the postwar years to discuss
what they had been through and some suffered life-
long medical issues.

What was common knowledge among the
Americans, but kept carefully from their captors,
was the American "sabotaging to beat hell" that
was taking place at the Mitsubishi factory. "They're
putting sand and shavings in the oil," Siggy recorded,
"dropping machines, parts, and tools accidentally.
Strangely enough, a lot of this equipment finds its
way to the [new] concrete foundation, which is being
laid down. The best story is the one about the new

lathe that disappeared. I believe if the Japs dig up the foundation it will be found. There also seems to be a lot of shovels disappearing." The factory management was probably aware of some of this, but to report too much of it to the camp commander would have led to trouble at that end—men punished and then unable to show up for work. One never knew how Colonel Matsuda's men would respond when angered: three Chinese men were summarily shot dead when it was discovered they had been passing extra cigarettes to the men in the camp.

Two surprises in March were the announcements that everyone in the camp would henceforth be paid a small salary, including the kitchen staff, just as the 500 American factory workers were, and that the men would be allowed to write a letter home. (There was a Catch-22 to the salary pay-outs. If a man wanted ciga-rettes, a new toothbrush, some soap or tooth powder, even a pencil, he had to pay his captors for it, so the money went right back into Japanese pockets.) The "generous" gesture to communicate with one's family, of course, came with plenty of strings attached.

The message was not to exceed twenty-five words, they were told, and would be carefully monitored. Once they had scribbled out a few lines, it would then be typed by the office personnel who knew English and all the men had to do was sign it. Everyone was expected to say that he was doing fine. A few clever correspondents ended by writing, "I'm well and happy but don't tell my wife" or "You're not a widow yet."

Whether they passed muster with the censors no one knew. Whether the letters all reached their destination isn't clear, either.

On April 1st, the order was issued that there were to be no more fires in the barracks. Winter was officially over—no matter what the actual temperature readings were, no matter if it still snowed—and that also meant everyone had to turn in the fur-lined shoes they had been given during the worst of the cold weather to be replaced by their regulation G.I. shoes. A hard-and-fast rule at the camp: POW's were allowed only one pair of shoes at a time, one coat, one shirt, one pair of pants, one pair of underwear, no doubling-up permitted. Men who had unthinkingly gotten rid of their coats or underwear because of their repulsive condition and lice infestation, expecting fresh clothes in the spring, now had to do without entirely. With the coming of spring, the meals seemed to become more watery as well, and an onslaught of mice and fleas had to be dealt with.

Some men felt they couldn't endure life in the camp anymore. Three men from Barracks 14 let it be known they were going to try to escape through the back fence. The barbed wire wasn't electrified as it would be later in the year when the camp was moved to a new site. "The boys tried to talk them out of it," Siggy wrote, "because of the long distance they would have to go to reach friendly territory and also because of the situation it would leave the rest of us in." They wouldn't listen. Finally, their barracks mates turned them in "for their own good and ours also." They were locked in the guardhouse.

Enduring the unendurable usually required finding pleasure in the smallest pursuits that would have been taken for granted in civilian life but meant everything in captivity. In the warmer weather, the men were allowed into the yard to play baseball or horseshoes, jump rope or hold wrestling matches, and they were even able to borrow a guitar from the main office to listen to someone in their barracks who knew how to play and to have singing contests. A British POW known for his good singing voice came by from time to time to entertain his American friends. To everyone's surprise, Butterball, the famed dog-killer, was particularly skillful on the guitar. Men came from other barracks to hear him play. The guitar was passed between barracks and taken away for a time when some officers were caught playing it after lights out.

(Siggy expresses no surprise in the diary that the Japanese would have had a guitar on hand to let the men use, though he and everyone else must surely have wondered about that. In fact, there were two guitars, two mandolins, two violins, an accordion, and six harmonicas available for POW use on Sundays. The origin of this musical trove wasn't something any American would have learned about until after the war. The explanation is clear-cut. The Vatican had given the Japanese 1,500 yen for medical supplies for the Manchurian camp. With stunning audacity,

Colonel Matsuda let the pope's representatives know
that recreational and musical equipment would be a
better use of the funds. Hence, the instruments.)

Making model airplanes out of pieces of ply-
wood became a big pastime in Siggy's barracks. He
and Teddy Olslager sat outside during good weather
whittling away with dull knives. The men who worked
in the factory brought back paints, sandpaper, cello-
phane, and glue for them to use. Some of the guards
looked as if they would like to have smashed their
prisoners' handiwork under their heels, but were
clearly under orders to leave it be, while others were
amused at the whole endeavor and the clever results,
especially when the men started to construct their
own airport in miniature. Colonel Matsuda came
by to have a look one day. He seemed to enjoy what
he saw, "but we made one mistake," Siggy admitted.
"Someone made a small American flag and had it
flying at the time [at their airport]. [The commander]
told us to take it down as this was the only American
flag flying in Manchuria. He also states that [our] flag
will never be flying in Manchuria."

Any gestures of humanity granted their prisoners
by the Japanese were very small in comparison to the
ongoing climate of deprivation and abuse. Men who
fell out of line in the morning, too sick to walk to the
factory in town, were forced back into place. It was a
matter of *go to work or take a beating that will make you
wish you had*. Malnutrition and dysentery continued
to claim lives. Men caught gambling at cards were

dragged off to the guardhouse or made to run around
the perimeter of the camp as many as forty times.
Shakedown inspections brought stern reprisals. "They
really ransacked the barracks. They pulled beds and
pillows apart," Siggy wrote. If any winter clothing
was found that was supposed to have been turned in,
or other contraband like sugar or sharp knives, the
guards refused to issue any more commissary supplies
until they were satisfied there was nothing more to be
found. Major Hankins as the senior American officer
wasn't much help. He told the kitchen staff to go easy
on the coal. "The way he talked, you'd think he was
paying for it," Siggy griped.

Siggy was one for horseplay. It's easy to get a
sense that he must have driven some of his work
and barrack mates crazy, putting bricks under their
mattress, having water fights with his co-workers in
the kitchen when no Japanese officers were around,
dropping lit cigarette butts into the coat pockets of
men who were looking away. He made up outrageous
nicknames for his bunk mates just to get their goat.
He wasn't the only one playing the prankster, but
he seems to have found anything that kept a sense
of numbness or depression at bay—anything that
elicited a response, even a pissed-off one—particularly important. He saw what happened to the men
who went blank. He saw what happened when men
retreated into themselves and lost the will to live. Like
his mother who enjoyed nothing so much as having
her Austrian lady friends over for coffee and strudel

of an afternoon, Siggy had an intense craving for social interaction. For conversation, for attention and friendship. He had never been a loner. That probably helped to save him.

In early June, he fell ill. He went to see the chief American medical officer, Mark Herbst, who took his temperature. It was 104. Even with a fever that high, the Japanese doctor on duty was opposed to admitting him to the hospital. Herbst argued vehemently with the man and finally saw to it that his patient was given a bed in a ward. That was the point of finding your way to Captain Herbst among all the medical personnel if something was wrong: he wasn't afraid to contradict his Japanese counterparts. He was even known on occasion to go directly to Colonel Matsuda with his complaints. The only medicine Siggy was given, though, was aspirin. Friends—Lee, Bosko, and others—came by with sugared tea, barracks gossip, the all-important results of the recent baseball games, and a book for the weary patient to look through; Lee shaved him.

Six days after being admitted to the hospital, Siggy was released, none the wiser for what had caused so debilitating a fever. The following day everyone in the camp was ordered out to the cemetery for some kind of memorial program. (The diary does not explain what that gravesite program was all about.) Siggy had a fit of vomiting there and struggled to make it back to his barracks—"weak as a kitten." Arnold Bocksel gave him permission to stay home from the kitchen for a few more days. Others covered for him. His on-again-off-again fever and digestive troubles plagued him throughout the summer.

A week after Siggy was released from the hospital, the unimaginable happened. Everyone woke to the news that three Americans had escaped during the night. No one was allowed to leave for work in the city. The Japanese, guards and officers, were beside themselves with rage. Everyone in the barracks where the men slept was interrogated, again and again, for anything they knew about the escape plan. One of the men, a Marine, named the Chinese contact in the city who had provided the three with a map. The word around the camp was that he was subsequently shot. (He was actually tortured and imprisoned but lived.) All the trees near the camp were cut down and more barbed wire was put up. Baseball games were forbidden; rations were cut. One day *tenko* was held at three a.m. to be sure everyone was present and accounted for, another at midnight. The guards seemed more than usually ready to slap a man or knock him to the ground, whether there was reason to or not. The animosity between captor and captive reached a new pitch.

Two weeks after their disappearance, the three men were back at the camp, barefoot and bedraggled. One had been shot in the arm and another had a bandage around his head. Apparently, they had reached the frontier of Mongolia, but everything had gone wrong at that point. They were kept out of sight for a few weeks, no doubt subjected to vicious abuse, and then shot and buried in unmarked graves near, but not in, the cemetery.

—◊◊◊—

Sex wasn't a topic that famished, beaten, vulnerable men thought or talked about very often, but it couldn't be said that everyone was oblivious to the need. The men who worked at the factory sometimes came back with stories of the beautiful Chinese women they had seen in Mukden. One man in the barracks whittled a statuette of a naked girl that caused a lot of discussion and even the guards wanted a look. An American corpsman who worked in the hospital started making advances on some of the younger, better-looking servicemen that summer, which Siggy was shocked to hear about. Captain Herbst got wind of it and put the man on night duty in the diarrhea ward to keep him out of trouble. Frank Gagliardi came back one night from work at the Utilities Shop and told Siggy about a Japanese guard who was making a play for some of the men. (A number of the guards were "queer," Siggy was sure.) An American medic he met later that year was referred to in his diary as someone who was "slightly eccentric...[and] would do good in Greenwich Village."

In a gruesome way everyone was reminded of the cost of unprotected sex when a Native American serviceman from New Mexico died that month. He had contracted syphilis in the Philippines almost two years earlier. Lacking access to antibiotics, he went without any treatment for all of his time on Bataan and in Manchuria. He was obviously near death when the doctors at the hospital tried curing him, Siggy wrote, "by injecting him with malaria germs to see if the malaria fever would kill the syphilis germs." Obviously, it did no good. The man was allowed to have an American flag draped over his coffin and permission was given to play taps. Colonel Matsuda, to everyone's astonishment, came to the brief service and bowed his head reverently.

The escape and recapture of the three men coincided with the visit of a propaganda team from Tokyo. They interviewed and tape-recorded some of the Americans, who kept their remarks as general as possible while they were being stared at by the intimidating Japanese officer they called among themselves "Bull of the Woods." The propaganda team filmed the bakery and the men diligently working at their respective jobs, playing baseball, and enjoying their musical instruments. They also filmed the oddly respectful funeral for the syphilitic serviceman—all part of an effort to show how humanely the POW's were being treated should any criticism be heard in neutral countries. Everyone in the camp, of course, was well aware of how their captors were stonewalling the Red Cross, refusing to let outside inspectors in, holding back vital medicine, and mistreating the Allied prisoners on a regular basis.

When Siggy's health didn't improve over the course of the summer, he went back to see Captain Herbst, who ran a blood test and told him he was suffering from anemia. "He told me to change jobs with someone at the camp," he wrote, "as to get away from the hot kitchen." Herbst said he would speak to Major Hankins and Arnold Bocksel. Frank Gagliardi promised to get Siggy assigned to work with him in the Utilities Shop. That transition would also entail sleeping in a different barracks: "I'm to be placed in the Air Corps section [out of the Special Duty section]. This is OK with me as most of my friends will be there." More and more, seeing one's friends made a difference in how the men accepted their lot.

Otherwise, rumors kept the men going—most of them that summer dead wrong, examples of misinformation unintentionally passed on by the Chinese at the factory, snippets misread from the Japanese magazines they were allowed to look at, or pure wishful thinking. All of it sounded encouraging—the Allies had retaken Norway, the Russians had pushed the Germans back to the border of Poland, Rangoon had been liberated, MacArthur was back in the Philippines—but none of those advances actually happened until late in the following year or early in 1945. The one rumor that was true was that a new camp had been prepared closer to the city and that everyone would be moved there in a matter of days.

On the 29th of July, the men were instructed to bring their mattresses and all of their personal effects to the parade ground to load those items onto the waiting trucks, keeping with them only their toothbrushes and blankets. Anticipating this, Siggy had hidden his diary and a few other contraband articles in the boxes of Utility Shop equipment. A wise move: when the men completed the two-hour walk to the new detention site, they were ordered to strip naked for an inspection of their body and clothes before they proceeded to their assigned barracks.

Siggy recorded in minute detail everything about the new camp: the eleven brick buildings with tile roofs, which included three two-story buildings for sleeping quarters, the twenty-two- room hospital, the morgue, kitchen, bakery, barber shop (one haircut a month allowed), water gallery, commissary, tailor and shoe shops, bath houses and guard house (with eight cells), the principal offices. The camp was encircled with a fifteen-foot wall topped by electrified barbed wire and four guard towers. In the lavatories, there were 27 toilets per 400 men. Conditions were appreciably better, he noted with relief, than at Camp O'Donnell, Camp Cabanatuan, or the first Mukden facility. He also made it his business to find out right away who had access to the camp's office supplies. He was running out of scraps of paper for his diary and needed someone to swipe enough for him to keep it going.

Settling in, the men heard an exciting rumor, which an English-speaking Japanese guard even confirmed for them, though he told them not to make too much of it, namely, that the Americans and British were fighting their way up the boot of Italy and Mussolini had fled Rome. That news was a cause for hope that the war in Europe wouldn't last forever and a more aggressive movement against Japan might follow. It also led to an absurd rumor out of nowhere: that Hitler had fled Germany and Rudolf Hess was now in charge of the Nazi government. After a while, Siggy—not alone among his barrack mates—grew impatient with the eagerness that some men were spreading rumors that had no basis in reality. They were raising false hopes. It was better to try not to imagine a date when their ordeal would be over and those still left standing could go home.

Siggy's first duties at the Utilities Shop involved making benches all day for use in the different shops, a task he labored over with Frank Gagliardi. Some Chinese workers were in the camp attempting to repair the pumps and motor in the boiler room that weren't working. When the guards weren't looking, they slipped them some buns "which they devoured immediately" as bread was a very scarce commodity in the city. The workers repaid the Americans with handfuls of cigarettes. Captain Herbst, who seems to have taken an interest in Siggy's well-being, came by to see how he was getting on.

The bad news about Siggy's new work assignment was that the Japanese command had determined that a payroll force of twelve men was all that could be allotted for the Utilities Shop, so Siggy—last hired, last paid—would be working without a salary for the foreseeable future. That at least spared him being involved in a ridiculous dust-up with one of the American officers who insisted on being saluted by the enlisted men when he handed out their pay envelopes. The men refused to do it. We're in a POW camp now, not on an American base or the streets of Manila, they maintained. That kind of misplaced officiousness infuriated the enlisted men. It was bad enough they had to acknowledge any Japanese officer they walked by, which wasn't done by a hand salute but, rather, a deep bow from the waist (and the men had to be prepared to be slapped if the bow wasn't low enough). They'd be damned, though, if they'd acknowledge the superior rank of one of their own officers—more well-fed than they were, to begin with—while living behind barbed wire. They insisted that General Ned King had told them back on Bataan that all Americans were in the same boat now as prisoners and that officers and enlisted men were one and the same until the liberation. When the American officer took his case to the Japanese, they sided with him. Some of the men still protested; the result was a camp-wide suspension of the already intermittent Sunday religious services, denial of any more books or reading matter, and a cut in cigarette rations from the commissary. And more short tempers and black eyes in the barracks.

In the new camp, Siggy observed an activity he worried about and wanted no part of but it often

involved his best buddies so he couldn't exactly look
the other way. Gambling, once an occasional end-of-
the-day pastime, became overnight a compulsion in
the new camp. On many days the minute men got
back to the barracks from their work detail, out came
the cards and the yen they had been paid and piles
of cigarettes or extra food or anything else that could
be thrown into the pot and they kept at it until lights
out. These weren't friendly blackjack or poker games,
either. The whole thing was cutthroat competitive
and led to some heated exchanges. Knowing that
Siggy had finally been put back on the Utilities Shop
payroll, his pals, especially Jack Lee and Nick Bosko,
pressed him for loans, loans they often couldn't pay
back because their lucky streaks were few and far
between. On one occasion, Lee and Bosko dropped
200 yen in one game, a substantial sum.

Siggy had the reputation of a soft touch. "They
want to cut me in as a partner for a small stake," he
noted, "but I told them no soap as gambling is out
of my line." Yet when pressed, he tended to advance
them money, especially if he got something in
return—say, a fresh bar of soap—that he wanted.

Even Teddy Olslager, whom Siggy thought of as
a steady guy, fell into the habit in a bad way. But his
situation was worse. The men who worked in the city
in the factory had started bringing back homemade
liquor in their canteens which they had purchased
from their Chinese co-workers. Teddy liked to imbibe.
That was dangerous enough, Siggy felt, but marijuana

also made its way back to the camp on occasion, and
Teddy was up for that, too. ("[He] said it made him
feel he was floating on air.") In general, the guards,
or some of them, seemed to care less about discipline
than they had at the first Mukden camp. Their crack-
down efforts could be brutal, but they could also
be more perfunctory. One night one of the guards
actually joined in a card game. He walked away with
110 yen. Other guards would break up a game and
drag some of the participants off to the guard house.
Inspections, always an erratic business, now became
more aggressive and pointless, with everything
thrown hither and yon, leaving their quarters looking
"as if a cyclone had struck it."

There were fewer guards around that fall as some
had been reassigned to fight at the front, a transfer
none of them welcomed. There were other clues
the POW's could pick up on that their captors were
becoming concerned about the progress of war and
nervous about Allied incursions into China. The men
were instructed to keep boxes of sand in the barracks
at all times (though Siggy wondered just what that
was supposed to do if they were hit by an incendiary
bomb), and machine gun pits and foxholes were being
dug outside the compound walls. A factory only half
a mile away mounted anti-aircraft guns on its roof.
One of the Americans noticed a stockpile of gas masks
in the supply room, and the number of air raid drills
and practice black-outs increased. As it became dark
earlier, *tenko* was held indoors. Many of the guards

were making efforts to learn English, taught by those
officers who were fluent.

Yet as the regimen became just slightly less
exacting and health concerns taken somewhat more
seriously—in October everyone was given an chest
X-ray to test for tuberculosis and a cholera vaccine
and men were allowed to purchase apples and pears
on work details outside the camp—and the commissary started to offer more goods for purchase (e.g.,
toilet paper, tea cakes, peanuts, candy), the prisoners
were themselves feeling the strain of more than a
year in captivity. Rugby and touch football games
became rougher, more brutal. Provocations between
men at work were getting worse. Men who didn't pay
their gambling debts were beaten up. Stealing in the
barracks continued. Siggy had no sooner washed
and deloused a blanket of his than it disappeared.
"White rats" (i.e., squealers) informed on others to
curry favor with the guards. ("We watch them like
hawks," Siggy commented.) Rumors angrily insisted
on by those who were spreading them—that FDR and
Tojo were meeting in Honolulu for talks, that the war
would be over in a matter of weeks and that the Nazi
government had fled Berlin—became more ludicrous
and far-fetched.

Men wanted out of jobs they felt were too onerous
and were willing to go to desperate lengths to do that.
Teddy Olslager was in the hospital. He had been working in the foundry at the factory and had had enough.
He asked a co-worker to take a sledgehammer to one

of his fingers. The fellow obliged. Siggy visited Teddy and was told the injury was worth it, that the rest in the hospital was "wonderful." Siggy didn't sound convinced and worried about the health of his friends. Frank Gagliardi had come down with malaria. Later he had two teeth inexpertly extracted without anesthesia that left painful splinters in his mouth. Jack Lee was losing too much weight. Every week they heard about someone they knew being carried to the morgue.

Some men became less cautious in the midst of this high level of stress. One morning "Bull in the Woods" gave a stern lecture about smoking in the lavatory and lined up five men and knocked each one down three times to make his point. "After this demonstration," Siggy wrote, "you would think the men would be a little more careful, but no. A few more were caught smoking at the factory this afternoon. They were thrown in the guard house for ten days [where they were made to do push-ups while being slapped until they collapsed on the floor]. The Bull stripped one middle-aged man of all his clothing, then put him in the guard house." The temperature at night hovered around thirty-two degrees. Pools of water amid the campgrounds were starting to freeze.

Given the addictive nature of smoking, and how little the men had to relieve their pain and frustration, it's understandable how a few stolen minutes with a cigarette became an urgent need for so many of the POW's. Men would hide them in their leggings or in the crotch of their underwear. It's interesting, too, that Siggy did his best not to let that craving overtake him. He was becoming more self-protective, more judicious. He used his every contact at the hospital to get him vitamins, cod liver oil, and aspirin that he could hide and stockpile for the coming winter. He asked Robert Rosendahl, who worked in the tailor shop, to make him a pair of gloves in anticipation of the cold. He knew that the tailor shop was overseen by the most lenient of the Japanese supervisors.

By his own account, Siggy was careful not ever to talk back to a guard or officer. His friend Jack Lee had done that and paid a terrible price, as he related it to Siggy later. He was made to stand at attention for hours at headquarters until a Lieutenant Miki, a particularly cruel man, came in and made him do push-ups until he was exhausted. Then he was forced to stand on his head with his feet pressed against a hot stove. He passed out. Miki revived him by pouring hot water from a tea kettle on his head. Then he was worked over with a bamboo stick by a few guards before he was let go, scalded and bruised.

Word of an equally distressing episode made the rounds of the camp in November. Caught gambling in their quarters at night, a group of Navy men were told to stand in two lines facing each other. Each man was made to slap the person opposite him in the face— hard. "This went on for five minutes," Siggy wrote. "If one man didn't slap hard enough, the Jap [guard] intervened and demonstrated."

In the meantime, Siggy's work in the Utilities Shop kept him busy all day. He was part of a team charged with installing coal stoves in the barracks, repairing broken windows, making wooden shoes for the men to wear in the bath house, and assorted other painting and woodworking tasks. In his own barracks, he showed his expertise at making a rat trap using wire and nails, devices that were becoming necessary as the rats grew bolder and climbed over the men in bed at night. Occasionally, when the kitchen staff were short-handed, he would go back to helping prepare the meals. They were more varied than they had been at the old camp—including now turnip soup, cole-slaw, beans, and maize paddies with a paste-like flour gravy—but never in sufficient quantity to fill anyone's stomach. Nor, with the amount of coal provided, were the stoves ever working in a way to keep anyone warm as winter approached. The cold could be literally killing. Lieutenant Miki's special punishment for anyone he wanted thrown in the freezing guardhouse was to see that they were kept there naked for days at a time. Most of those men ended up in the hospital with pneumonia, some too late to have a chance at recovery. About Miki, Siggy wrote, "When and if we are freed, I hope someone of us gets to settle a few scores....Hanging's too good for him." No one was sorry when he was reassigned and left the camp in December. (He wasn't hanged, but Lieutenant—then Captain—Toru Miki was tried by a Chinese court in 1946 and sentenced to twenty-five years at hard labor.)

Everything at the camp followed Japanese military protocol. The men were told at what date they could begin to wear the woolen underwear they were given. Permission to put on the woolen stockings and gloves was withheld until the officially approved date somewhat later. The same was true with their winter coats and when fires indoors could be started. At the same time, it appeared that more guards were open to being bribed to look the other way. One American was said to have "the liquor business all sewed up," with several bottles coming in a day. To keep warm, Siggy took his share when offered. Even a few of the American doctors at the camp hospital and more than a few of the kitchen staff were showing up to work half bombed.

Emboldened, the men started to refuse certain extreme commands. When they were ordered to scoop out the overflowing toilets, a regular occurrence, they wouldn't do it. "In the past," Siggy noted, "the Japs had Chinamen come in to do it. We call them 'honey dippers' as they make it their occupation. This refusal has the Japs stumped. They haven't done anything about it as yet. Boy," he concluded, "we even have strikes in prison camp."

True initiative was shown by the Americans about the medicine that was being withheld. Men working at the factory started surreptitiously buying significant quantities of medicine from the Chinese there. The American doctors decided to start a common bank. The set-up: "When a man gets sick, he goes to sick call and if the Jap doctor does not give him medicine, the

American doctor gives him a slip on the QT. The man presents this slip to the barracks leader who gives him the medicine." This cost money, of course. So each man in the barracks was leaned on to give twenty sen to start a common fund. (A sen was a fractional part of a yen, not a large sum to ask for.) Eventually, every man in the camp was hit up for twenty sen, larger amounts when needed to keep the system going. The medicine bank soon had a fund of 3,000 yen. Siggy speculated that at one point the Americans had a hidden supply of pharmaceuticals larger than what the Japanese were hoarding themselves in the camp hospital. Yet it was never enough.

Siggy himself showed initiative with the medicine, cigarettes, or liquor that came his way that winter, stockpiling it and selling it to anyone willing to pay a fair mark-up but keeping some back for his friends. He did an especially brisk business with bars of soap the heavy drinkers gave him in return for a bottle who then later wanted to buy back their own soap. He was "the Jew Boy," an operator, to the men in the boiler room and the barracks who heard about his transactions. There were some who resented the number of hot baths he managed to cadge at the hospital. "A man with real friends will pull through this mess with flying colors," he wrote. If he didn't adopt a you-scratch-my-back-I'll-scratch-yours approach to camp life, he was sure he'd "probably be with the rest of the unfortunates in the Cabanatuan graveyard." Passivity led to the morgue, to the graveyard.

—ᴧᴧ—

The plan for Christmas dinner was to cook some pheasants. One American doctor, who was allowed to go into Mukden, was given the money to purchase the pheasants. Siggy put up 80 yen. The guards had indicated they wouldn't take notice. The problem: the man had become a serious alcoholic. He evidently spent the money he was entrusted with for liquor, the same way he had sold his own ring and watch to get his hands on a bottle. Liquor was becoming an out-of-control issue. On Christmas Eve, some of the men were, as Siggy put it, "drunken goons." The smell of weed, for that matter, was becoming hard to miss.

That evening and the following night, the men were pretty much left on their own. A musical program for anyone who wanted to attend on the former occasion was held in the British section of the camp— with men performing a skit dressed as women with female clothing smuggled in from the factory—and in the American Air Force section on the night of Christmas Day. "We ended each program by displaying the American and British flags, also by singing each national anthem." (The flags were confiscated the next week when word got out about that.) Everyone in the guard house had been let out for the day. On New Year's Eve, permission was given to keep the lights on until midnight.

In the new year, the Japanese command and the factory management decided it was time to have a new contingent of POW's sent to work in Mukden. Siggy was on the list to be moved from Utilities to factory work, which was the last thing he wanted—the work was arduous and the walk there in the cold was debilitating. Captain Herbst saw that his name was taken off the list on the basis of his erratic health and weight loss. The number of bed-ridden pneumonia patients was growing.

Finally, the Japanese agreed to release some of the packages that had been sent from the U.S. via the Red Cross and some of the letters written to the men from home. The mail was distributed piecemeal by state over a period of several weeks, starting with anyone from Texas and New York. It was perfectly obvious when the boxes were opened that their captors had first gone through them, taking what they wanted, like the better clothing, leaving what they didn't, which included items such as shaving supplies. There was nothing for Siggy that month, but he did record—in a sadly matter-of-fact way—that on January 15, 1944, he was slapped across the face by an angry guard for not standing at attention, presumably during *tenko*. A new edict was also issued that month about bringing into camp any contraband items from the factory. The funneling of liquor, cigarettes, medicine, marijuana, and clothes from the city was about to be radically curtailed, or so the Japanese intended. "Bull of the Woods" said he would strip every man naked in the freezing cold and have them searched as they came back from work before being allowed into the camp if it didn't stop.

Even with that dire threat, some men couldn't do without their liquor. Bottles were too easy to spot under a coat, but ripping out the inside of a basketball or football and using that material as a bladder pressed under one's shirt next to the skin, in effect a pocket that could be filled with liquid and tied up, seemed to be an alternative worth trying. Siggy was droll about that development: "So far this method has proved satisfactory."

At last, in February, men from the New England states were called down to the office to receive their packages. The guard doing the distributing looked as if he expected a hand-out. "The bastard didn't get anything from me," Siggy wrote. His haul from his family was recorded with great exuberance: two cans of meat, one bottle of vitamins, two sets of shorts and undershirts, three pairs of socks, one sewing kit, one shaving kit, one box of prunes, one box of raisins, one bottle of Nestle's, chewing gum, cigarettes, a leather belt, handkerchiefs and candy. Two letters soon followed, the first news he had had since before Pearl Harbor. They were postmarked 1942. Everyone was well, his mother wrote. They thought about him all the time. He read the letters through a hundred times, he said.

Siggy was sometimes delegated to join the men who made the thin wood coffins, always a depressing duty. When he and a friend from the Utilities Shop, John Koot, a Pennsylvania farm boy (and another son of a native-born Austrian), finished the job for one recently deceased fellow, they brought it to the hospital and helped one of the orderlies place the body inside. Then they nailed it shut. The smell of gangrene was fierce. The American doctor in charge looked as if he had been crying. They were told to see that it was brought to the cemetery first thing in the morning.

The situation in the hospital wasn't anything to inspire hope. The doctor who had tried to save the soldier they just buried was evidently finding the conditions and workload unbearable as he was "half in the bag" a lot of the time, Siggy had noticed. The medical team had to make do, as always, without the medicine and equipment they needed. Another soldier almost lost his entire hand to an infection that turned gangrenous. All the doctors could do was to save the hand itself and one finger.

Just as infuriating was the show their captors sometimes put on for the funeral of one of the Allied prisoners. The very fact of the funeral, the flag-draped coffin, the small pulpit next to it for a few words of prayer and eulogizing, the officers (American, British, and Japanese) looking mournful—it was perfectly obvious when the cameras went off, that they were in the midst of a propaganda ploy with the photographs to be reproduced in Japanese papers showing the civilized treatment their forces accorded the enemy.

Closer to everyday reality, the same week as the funeral of the gangrene victim, was the punishment meted out to two men who had answered back to their guards. They were made to run around the parade ground twenty times, then to stand with their arms extended and knees bent until they collapsed on the ground. After this, they were dragged inside and had to crawl on their hands and knees doing a figure 8 in and out under a table. "This went on all afternoon," Siggy wrote. "It made your blood boil to watch them, especially when they started kicking the men for not going fast enough." Another punishment for lesser offenses resulted in a haircut that shaved the men bald but left a tuft of hair in the center of the head. Physical abuse and humiliation: they were equally effective, the Japanese officers felt, in reminding the Americans and the British who was in charge.

Those packages were a godsend, though. Nick Bosko on kitchen duty said he would use the prunes and raisins Siggy had received from home to bake a pie for him, which he did. Siggy shared it with three others, including Frank Gagliardi. It was so good that Siggy decided to make an effort to buy more prunes and raisins from anyone in the camp who could get some in Mukden to have another pie. With just over 600 men going out each day to the factory in the city, and some going to smaller factories nearby including one that produced leather goods, the odds of that were fair to good. Despite the best efforts of the guards to stop the smuggling back into camp of assorted contraband, it still went on.

Drinking was becoming common enough to lead to a mass threat made to the entire camp in March. One man had stumbled back from the factory obviously intoxicated. He was thrown in the guard house. At *tenko* that night, they were told that if the other men he had been drinking with did not come forward and give themselves up by lights-out at 9:30, everyone would pay a price. At 9:30, with no one admitting to anything, everyone was told to assemble outside without their coats. You will stand here all night, Lieutenant Ando—one of the most detested officers—told them, until I get the answer I want. Thirty minutes passed in the chill air. It started to snow. "Then he started getting mad. First, he drew his saber, then walked up and down the ranks looking for someone to make a false move. At 11:30, three men stepped out of line and gave themselves up." Siggy later heard that some of the British officers had at first refused to leave their barracks and stand in the cold, "but changed their minds when they had a bayonet stuck in their ribs."

Siggy himself had a close call when he looked under the stairs in his barracks where he had stashed his diary and some detailed maps he had drawn of Cabanatuan. Someone had taken the maps. He had to worry that if it was a "white rat" who had done the pilfering, he might be vulnerable to being reported to the guards. Though his name didn't appear anywhere on the diary, it would be clear enough from the contents who the author was. He moved his diary to a new hiding place in the Utilities Shop—not that the shop was the safest place. John Koot had had eighty yen stolen that he had squirreled away there.

The last days of winter saw Siggy brought low
by the flu and a sinus infection. Nonetheless, when
exempted from work, he dragged himself to the
bakery to sit for long stretches of time as it was the
warmest place in the camp. He was also worried about
worms. Almost half the men in the camp seemed to
have them. Everyone had heard about a man named
Martin from his section who had actually coughed
up two white worms about twelve inches long and
the diameter of a pencil. Hemorrhoids were another
complaint. The men with the most egregious cases,
aggravated by the diarrhea that seemed to burden
everyone every several days, had to be operated on in
the hospital by the well-meaning but hard-drinking
American doctor, assisted by a Japanese physician
who stood by just to watch the procedure, having
admitted that he knew nothing about how to perform
the operation but was willing to give it a try in the
near future.

Siggy and the others who suffered from that
painful condition, but who had no intention of letting
anyone operate on them, spent a half hour each night
in the barracks soaking their bottoms in a bucket
of hot water. Privacy and dignity had long gone by
the wayside.

Spring allowed for more time outside in the fresh
air, but that did nothing to lessen the tensions that
were building up in the barracks. "A Yank and a Limey
had a fight in front of Barracks 3," Siggy observed at
the end of April. "A second Limey tried to stop the

fight, [but] another Yank stepped in and grabbed the
second Limey. This was the beginning of a big gang
fight"—a riot. Things were getting out of hand until
someone yelled "Air raid!" which was the camp-wide
code to alert everyone that the guards were on their
way. The mob dispersed to their own bunks—to gripe,
drink, gamble, and smoke.

A new factory opened up down the road from
the camp that made steel parts for bridges. The men
who were assigned there said that the work was
strenuous, but that they were pretty much left alone
all day and they were allowed more food because of
the hard nature of their work. They had also noticed
some young Japanese women working in the office
who seemed friendly. "Good contacts," they hoped—
particularly for the purchase of more cigarettes.
Cigarettes at times edged out liquor as the must-have
commodity. One desperate British serviceman had
been caught coming back from Mukden with sixty
packs of smokes on him.

Outwitting the guards and being apprised of
the timing of the next inspection became more
important all the time. But now there was a system in place. A white towel in the center window of
Barracks 2 alerted the men coming back from the
factory that "Bull of the Woods" or another officer
like him was on duty that night, meaning that trying
to smuggle anything in was going to be very risky.
"If nothing is showing," Siggy wrote, "[you] use your
own discretion."

Men were being interviewed throughout the spring to form a work detail that was going to be sent to the leather factory a good distance away. No one really wanted to be assigned to this new duty, not knowing what the living conditions or the work would be like, and though he was interviewed twice, Siggy's health ultimately kept him off the final list. Thirty-two men were told to pack up everything in the last week of May and be prepared to leave the camp on short notice. Another detail was organized the following day, this time involving 150 men, and no one had any idea where they would be going or for what purpose, but as it involved a train ride, they assumed it was in Korea or Japan. Siggy's friend Jack Lee was included with that group. Siggy slipped him some money to hide in the bottom of his tooth powder can. "Hope the Japs don't find it," he worried, "as he may need it wherever he's going." Everyone had an uneasy feeling about what this gradual dispersal of their numbers might mean. Teddy Olslager was sent off to a tannery factory. Siggy just had time to wish him good luck.

One thing on the minds of the Japanese was the growing fear of illness and contagion as the weather turned stiflingly hot. Everyone in the camp was hurriedly given another typhoid shot. The needles, probably reused many times, were "dull as hell." An edginess was starting to pervade camp life. Siggy saw his friend Frank Gagliardi beaten by "Bull of the Woods" on the arms and shoulders with the flat side of an ax and, when he stood up, smacked across the

back with a four-foot-long plank of wood—for a pre-
sumed infraction that turned out when investigated
to be no infraction at all. It was this kind of thing, he
wrote, "that makes my blood boil. I could kill him
without batting an eye lash."

Letters from home and packages from the Red
Cross continued to be a lifeline. Siggy received fifteen letters in one fell swoop, all postmarked the year
before. He was relieved to read that a close friend from
the old neighborhood, Billy Swensk, was back in New
Britain. He had been in the Philippines when Siggy
was there but had left for duty in Australia just before
Pearl Harbor, a close call. The Red Cross cartons were
suddenly coming in by the truckload, packed with
coffee, cheese, butter, jam, chocolate bars, raisins,
prunes, and powdered milk, though the Japanese officers took their sweet time distributing any of it.

A service for the dead was held out at the cemetery. Twenty-five men were picked to attend. They
came back discouraged at the condition of the graves,
some covered by grass that was knee-deep.

—◊◊◊—

June 6, 1944: a momentous day in Normandy and back
in the United States, but it was nothing anyone in
the camp got wind of until later in the week. Siggy's
note that day in his diary, the contents of which were
becoming more terse each week, as if he were running out of energy with the whole endeavor, simply

recorded the fact that he had agreed to switch places with another man and take kitchen duty for ten days. It was a sucker's move, he decided after a few days, as "the kitchen is a sweat box." Other entries that week simply review the day's rarely varying menu, log someone's passing ("One man died today. Had heart trouble."), or comment on the going-rate for cigarettes ("selling for 5 yen for ten").

The word the men received about D-Day later wasn't entirely uplifting. They heard through the "bamboo grapevine" that three-quarters of the Allied landing party were casualties (an erroneous bit of information), and too many false rumors over the months had dampened any excitement anyone could feel about events halfway around the world. Of more immediate concern was the report of an outbreak of cholera and dysentery in Mukden and the first cases of mumps appearing at the camp.

Siggy was relieved to get back to the Utilities Shop. He hadn't the stamina anymore for work in the kitchen. Keeping one's weight up, having the fortitude to get through the day, fighting the sluggishness that led to despair and weakened the will to live: it was a dreary, unending struggle. When he took part in the baseball games, he found he was too weak to run around the bases as he used to. He was certain, though, that he was going to be put on the list for yet another work detail being sent out of the camp. If that came to pass, "I have to find a way of disposing of this diary," he wrote, "as it is getting too bulky to handle."

This is where the false bottom of the soybean can came into use. Frank Gagliardi agreed to look out for it if Siggy was sent away and find a way to get it back to him eventually.

Siggy was right. He was leaving the camp with the new work detail of 175 men. They were going to a textile and clothing factory, a half-hour drive away. Living conditions were primitive. About six of the twelve showers worked, and the latrine, very near the dining area, consisted of seven rectangular holes and two urinals. The food was no better than at the main camp and heat was minimal when the weather turned cold. The men's work schedule, they were told, would be ten hours a day with one day off every two weeks. They were divided into two groups, those who were to help in getting the run-down facility into working order and those who were to learn to use the weaving machines. Siggy was put to work making wooden shoes alongside a friend, Hardy Bradley, and the local Chinese men who had been pressed into service. Bradley was a fellow student with Siggy when a Latino serviceman, James Lopez, offered to teach them some Spanish in their spare time.

The Japanese civilians who ran the factories near the camp were no better than their countrymen in uniform. When some of the Americans engaged in a work stoppage after being pushed beyond their limits, the vice president of the factory had them line up while they listened to him harangue them about the need to labor for the betterment of the Greater

East-Asia Co-Prosperity Sphere, after which he
started to smack the men across their faces with a belt.
In a rage, one of the Americans threw his canteen at
him. He was taken outside "tied to a post and given a
merciless belting." After that, his face "looked like a
piece of raw meat."

The Japanese military officials who heard about
this weren't pleased. They let the factory management
know that only the Army had the authority to punish
the prisoners and that anyone refusing to work should
be sent back to the camp where he would be properly
disciplined. The others in the group that had been
pummeled had welts across their faces, and a few of
them suffered infections as a result. Everyone at the
factory had their rations reduced that week.

Siggy benefited from that policy when a factory
manager grabbed him by the arm and tried to push
him, after he had complained about the unheated area
he was working in. He closed his fist and indicated
he'd strike back if attacked. The manager turned and
walked away. The Chinese workers liked seeing the
Americans stand up to their captors and slipped them
some liquor from time to time. On another occasion,
the Americans staged a sit-down strike demanding
more heat. The officer sent from the camp checked
the temperature, agreed that it was too cold, told the
management to provide more heat, and left—to the
Americans' surprise—with everyone unpunished.

When the shipments of fresh Red Cross clothing
came in in November, there weren't enough shirts,

pants, and socks to go around. The men drew lots
when it came time to distribute the goods. One person
in desperate need of new clothes was Hardy Bradley,
Siggy's shoe-making partner. Bradley developed a
case of dysentery so severe he couldn't control his
bowels and could barely walk. Siggy had to wash all
of his clothes for him every day until he was finally
transferred back to the hospital at the camp. He also
took over Bradley's other, part-time job in the factory's
library, a room stocked—incongruously—with books
in English on Japanese art, Japanese music, Japanese
history, and how-to-learn-Japanese texts. Bradley
appreciated the help. When he returned from the
hospital a month later, he had a surprise Christmas
present for Siggy: the canteen with his diary in the
false bottom.

On December 28, 1944, Siggy reported a siren
going off at 11:00 in the morning and the Americans
being rushed back to their quarters outside the factory. (Writing this part of his journal from memory a
year-and-a-half later, Siggy confused the date: it was
December 7, 1944, not December 28th.) "Some of the
men managed to get a look out the windows and saw
white streaks in the sky," he wrote. "Then we knew
[our] "Boys" were here. The air raid lasted about an
hour." When the men excitedly went back to work in
the afternoon, their Chinese counterparts looked just
as happy. They hoped, too, that their liberation was
only a matter of time now that the tide in the Pacific
had turned.

That air raid that had initially thrilled the Americans wasn't entirely an occasion for celebratory feelings. It had had a sad, entirely unintended result. Though international law dictated that any sites where POWS were located were to be clearly marked as such so that pilots from the air could know that, the Japanese hadn't done anything to designate that the Mukden camp was a detention site. The American pilots heading toward the munitions plants in the area had no way of knowing that their countrymen were prisoners at the buildings they were flying over. They unloaded a bomb on the Mukden camp. Seventeen Americans were killed outright, two died later, and thirty-six were in the hospital in serious condition. Some men had lost arms and legs. The Japanese officer in charge of the work detail at the textile factory provided the men with the names of those who had died or been injured. Everyone knew someone among the dead and the injured.

All of the men were told they could make out wills after this event if they wished. They would be kept in the office. Siggy wrote his out to the effect that all his back pay and insurance was to go to his parents with the exception of $2,000 to be divided between his two sisters. The $1,000 to go to Marion was "to be used to give her a good start on her education," he hoped. He wondered about the family, how they were doing.

—◊—

Life had gone on at home, as it had to. The week of that air raid was the week Virginia Schreiner had accepted a proposal from a man she'd been dating for two years, who'd been granted a month's leave from the service.

The wedding was necessarily rushed. It took place three days after Christmas. The man she was marrying was a sailor from New Britain, Edward Loughery, who only several weeks earlier had spent three days on a raft in the Pacific after the sinking of his escort carrier, the *U.S.S. Gambier Bay*, in the Battle of Leyte Gulf. Josepha made her daughter's white wedding dress, stockpiled food coupons from anyone who would share, and prepared a breakfast of her specialties (her famous strudel) at her home for some of the guests and the bridal party. She was pleased that her daughter seemed so happy. Alois and the neighbors shoveled out the walk and driveway after the massive snowstorm the night before.

Marion at fourteen was a mature-looking bridesmaid along with Edward's two adult sisters (one of whom, Helen, was a nurse and Navy lieutenant), and the reception following the Mass at St. Peter's Church was held at a small lodge on a country road in the nearby town of Berlin not far from the train station. In the few photographs of that wintry day, Alois beams with pride amid the heaps of snow; Josepha looks happy in a few pictures, but appears more stoic than joyous in others.

After a honeymoon week in New York City, Virginia returned to Ellis Street and her typist's job at the Travelers Insurance Company in Hartford and Edward to active duty on the West Coast. Their letters from those post-honeymoon days apart are intense, passionate, both coy and remarkably explicit, and hopeful about a long and happy future together. It didn't quite work out that way.

Friends and relatives were sympathetic about the sadness and uncertainty the Schreiners were experiencing, and the Gold Star emblem in the front window of the house that told of a family who had lost a son or was mourning a P.O.W.'s unknown fate. Not everyone in New Britain displayed the empathy one would expect in those difficult circumstances, though. A store owner on nearby South Main Street made a pointed remark to Virginia one day on her nighttime air-raid warden's watch. "The Japs are probably treating your brother better, you know," he told her, "because you're German." She was too enraged to reply.

Any answer to that statement about her brother's treatment—a full awareness of the horror Siggy had endured for three and a half years—had to wait until the fall of 1945 when the family had their first sight of their emaciated, malarial, and deeply troubled Siggy.

There was one aspect of the man's callous remark that might have had some unintended truth to it, though, and even Siggy and his family wondered about it after the war. It wasn't only his good sense

in hiding from his captors the anger and disdain he
felt that saw him get by. It was, potentially, something
very different.

The ethnic background of Prisoner 124 wouldn't
have meant anything to his captors—an American
was an American, no matter where his ancestors
had come from—but Siggy's appearance might have
been what spared him from some of the worse abuse
other men endured. On one or two occasions, he
had wondered why one or another guard seemed
to take a liking to him, or at least not inflict on him
with any regularity the verbal abuse and random
beatings so many men had to take. It's true that he
never attempted to escape or got caught smuggling
contraband, but the more obvious explanation is
purely physical.

Siggy was short—as short as some of his captors,
and his complexion wasn't pale; it was more a dark
tan. And he had a vaguely Eastern European or even
Asiatic cast to his features. If the five-foot-eleven
blonde farm boy from Nebraska or the obviously
Jewish or southern or western American was the
desired target for a Japanese private who wanted
someone to take his own anger out on, Siggy usually
wasn't that person. Not that there weren't times when
he was in serious jeopardy as his own patience with
his situation wore thin.

The one time he fell seriously afoul of one of the
guards had to do with a sixteen-year-old Japanese kid
at the factory. More and more of the older Japanese

guards had been drafted back into service to fight
the American approach to the islands near Japan.
Teenage boys were being sent to China to take their
place. Among themselves, the Americans called the
kid assigned to the textile factory by the term for
"small boy" in Japanese. When he heard them one
day, he came at Siggy, who had been one of the offend-
ers, "with blood in his eyes. I held him off by having
my arms outstretched." Siggy continued: "The Jap Sgt.
we call 'Babyface' saw the kid in trouble, came over
and started slapping me. He was trying to knock me
down but was unable to do so. But when he started to
unhook his saber, I fell down on the next blow." After
"Babyface" left on his rounds, the kid crept up behind
Siggy and hit him in the back of his head with a water-
filled canteen. He almost passed out from the force
of the blow. He started for his attacker but another
guard intervened. "If I get a chance, I'll get even with
that kid someday," he wrote. He was transferred then
to a different job for a while, sweeping the floors of
the factory.

—∿—

Though he had his diary back in his possession in
December, Siggy found it almost impossible to continue writing in it that winter and spring. He was
exhausted, the fear of discovery while living at the
textile factory was a possibility, and there was less
and less to say as the grinding monotony of the days

dragged on. Only the hope of liberation kept the men going, and there were signs, finally, that they might not have to wait too long.

By May, the rumor mill had it that Germany had surrendered, which meant, everyone hoped, more of an Allied push in the Pacific now. They heard that the Philippines had been liberated and the Americans were getting closer to the Japanese homeland all the time. Everyone noticed that the guards, looking worried, had their ears glued to the radio all the time and their officers seemed less concerned each week with production goals at the factories. The Chinese workers at the factory were getting bolder, another encouraging sign. They started making knives out of files they'd been able to steal. They gleefully showed the Americans when no one was looking what they'd do to the Japanese when the time came.

It couldn't come soon enough for Siggy. After his floor-sweeping assignment, he was put to work in the weaving department. "We work without shirts but we're still sweating like pigs. In the winter time, the lint is not too tough to take but now it sticks to your body. Gets in your nose driving you nuts." Like all of his fellow workers, Siggy did his best to sabotage the machinery in subtle ways and then spend hours repairing it and ignoring his production quota. Eventually, the management tied ever-increasing quotas to the amount of food their workers were given. Men stopped working, became more sullen and defiant.

An American named Russell got caught writing "God Bless America" on a piece of canvas he was working on. (As the Mukden camp records list three Americans with that last name, it isn't possible to know which of the three Russells that Siggy is referring to. When he could, he identified a fellow prisoner by his first name as well.) The lieutenant in charge worked himself into a frenzy, hitting Russell so excitedly that he almost lost his balance, and then called on other guards to continue the beating. They made him stand at attention afterwards and that afternoon he was trucked back to the main camp and put in the guardhouse.

Siggy had to pay the price once for something someone else had done. He came out of the latrine and stopped to look at the production chart on the wall. Someone had just thrown a piece of oil-soaked waste material against it. Siggy was caught by the guards in a round-up with three other men, one of whom was the culprit. All of them denied knowing anything about the infraction, but their interrogator, Lieutenant Hayashi, finally decided it was Siggy who had done it. He started slapping him with his hand, then grabbed a ruler on his desk and used that, and then took a bamboo stick to the top of Siggy's skull. Worse followed.

Siggy was told to go outside to the yard and, if he was still insisting he was innocent, find the man who had done it. Sixty or so men were lined up with the three other suspects to the side. "[Hayashi] made me go up to each man," he wrote, "and ask if he did it. If the man answered 'No,' I was to slap him. I slapped 60 odd men....After this, he gave us another speech. This time screaming at the top of his lungs. Then he went around hitting each man on the top of his head with the bamboo stick." They were told they'd all stand there without food or water until someone confessed. Six hours later, the guilty party stepped forward. Siggy couldn't eat his dinner that night as the inside of his mouth was raw and bloody from the slaps of the ruler.

No one heard anything about the American victory at Okinawa or the dropping of the atomic bomb on Hiroshima and Nagasaki that summer. It was clear what was happening, though, when the men were told their work at the factory was done and they'd be returning, on foot, to the main camp that afternoon. They could see that files from the office were being burned. The men were told they had to leave any papers of their own behind, which made Siggy glad that the diary was well-hidden as he lost ten letters from home and two photos of the family enclosed in their last letters.

—∞—

Back at the main camp, the men from the different factories where they had been working were reunited with their friends and old barracks mates. "Everyone was comparing rumors," but they didn't have to wait long. On August 15th, Emperor Hirohito announced on the radio that Japan had accepted the Allied terms of surrender. General George Parker, who had some time before been transferred to the Mukden camp and replaced Major Haskins as the senior officer, read a statement telling the men of the armistice but warning them to be careful as word of this development was slow in getting out to the Japanese in China and that their captors still had their weapons. No one was to leave camp yet. The men were now under the "control and protection" of the Japanese. The Russians were expected soon from the north.

On the day after the Emperor's announcement, an American team of parachutists landed about two miles from the camp. They had brought supplies but also documentation about the ending of hostilities. (Only later did the POW's learn that they hadn't been believed at first and had been beaten and almost killed. They had also been sent to be sure that no atrocities occurred at the camps now that Japan was defeated. Siggy heard later in the week from Frank Gagliardi that more machine guns had recently been brought into the camp. No one needed to be told what that was all about. Some of the Chinese had told the Americans that if the officers were ever separated from the enlisted men, that would be the sign to make a break for it.)

On the evening of August 20th, the first Russians arrived at the camp. "Two staff cars came through the main gate. Some Russian officers disembarked, ignoring the Jap officers. They came right into the compound and waited until all the men in camp had assembled in front of the hospital stairs." A captain spoke through an interpreter, one of the former prisoners, a sergeant who knew Russian. "From this moment, you are free," the Russian officer told the men. "With this everyone busted out with a big howl." They replaced their former guards as guards them- selves, taking up their weapons from them. Colonel Matsuda surrendered his sword to General Parker that evening, with the men cheering at the sight of his humbling posture. Siggy skipped that ceremony to break into the Japanese soldiers' warehouse and scrounge about for new and better clothing, which he found along with a pair of sneakers.

A number of the former guards were put in the guard house. After midnight, one of the Americans went into the cells and "worked one of the Japs over."

The immediate changes in conditions were des- perately needed. Meals improved. Locals brought in eggs, fresh vegetables, and meat every day, paid for with money found in Colonel Matsuda's office—along with thousands of undelivered letters from the U.S., some of it two years old. (This is when Siggy learned to his surprise that his sister had been married eight months earlier.) The bath house was kept open every day. Air drops with more food, candy, tobacco, and medical supplies started that week. Doctors began to give injections to everyone in the camp, fearful of the spread of any number of diseases. By the end of the month, movie equipment and films were brought in to be shown every night.

Some men, like Siggy, began to recover relatively quickly once they were given three full meals a day, enough to drink, and freedom from their exhausting labors. Other men, barely able to get out of bed, weren't going to be able to come and go as they pleased for a long time. They would need to be the first to be evacuated when the Americans arrived.

Men in limited numbers were allowed to leave the camp to go into the city. Teddy Olslager had confiscated two bicycles from the Japanese guards so he and Siggy could be among an early group to go into Mukden . One of the first things Siggy was intent on doing was finding a photography shop and having his picture taken to send home. He was the worse for wear but alive, very thin but not as facially emaciated as some of the other, taller men in the camp, and proud of the pencil-thin moustache he had grown. He was photographed only from the neck up. His torso would have shown no belly and every protruding rib.

For some of the men in the camp who were ambulatory and even frisky, like Siggy, there was suddenly time, energy, and occasion for letting loose. At the announcement of the Japanese surrender, everyone had run about the camp into every building scavenging for souvenirs. Siggy claimed a saber he brought home with him. Then, on August 27th, he wrote, "Word went through [the] camp that a brewery was on the other side of town." The men were ecstatic, and there was no stopping them. "We invaded the place in full force, taking every available case of beer back to camp. About half of the men were in the bag before they reached the camp....It was a scream to see a cart going down the street loaded with 30 to 40 cases of beer with a few Americans on top, drunk as fools, hollering at the Chinks as they went by. That night... three quarters of the men in camp were drunk." Some who had stayed behind in town weren't in the mood to head back right away. They commandeered a Mukden fire truck and drove it through the streets, blasting the siren and screaming at nervous Chinese passersby. "Hog wild" was Siggy's description of the atmosphere.

More ominously, the Chinese were becoming less restrained all the time, with the Russians doing their best to calm them down even as they abused them themselves at times. Shops in town were being looted regardless of commodity or ownership. Rival Chinese gangs took to the streets, becoming bolder and more violent. The slashed bodies, both of fellow Chinese and the hated Japanese civilians, lay untouched in city's alleys for days. The city felt less safe all the time and, though it was highly unlikely that anyone would assault an American or a Russian, the breakdown of order was escalating. "I hope we get out of Mukden soon as things are getting hot," Siggy nervously concluded. Public services like the streetcar system had ceased to function, leaving the streets packed with bicycles, rickshaws, and horse-drawn carriages as the only way to get around. What Siggy and his fellow

Americans had no way of knowing at the time was that their Russian "liberators" and ostensible "allies" were not to be trusted. Some drunken Americans never made it back to camp; they were picked up and sent north to help in rebuilding the Soviet Union after the Nazi onslaught. The men who went into Mukden had done so, unknowingly, at great risk.

Siggy talked to one of the Americans who had been at the textile factory with him. He had gone back to see how things stood there. He said the place was a mess. Production had ceased, and their old barracks had been vandalized. The factory had been cleaned out of canvas, which was now being peddled furiously by the Chinese on the city's black market. Some of the Japanese guards had been knifed and slashed by the Chinese workers and left on the factory grounds to bleed to death.

The atmosphere in Mukden in those final weeks before Siggy was transported out was an incongruous blend of the menacing and the surreal. Siggy and Teddy Olslager hitched a ride into town and walked into the classy Mukden Club, a well-appointed building where a number of missionaries had been incarcerated during the war. No one stopped them. They'd heard there was a bowling alley there. They wanted to bowl. They took off their shoes, grabbed a set of pins and balls, and played. They left some food with the missionaries, who looked as if they'd had a hard time of it. Two days later he visited the convent in the city where some nuns had been confined for the entirety of the war. They wanted to say hello to the nuns, who looked pale and thin. They handed over packs of cigarettes to the no-doubt startled women, telling them to sell them for food if conditions didn't improve soon. Siggy attended a balalaika concert followed by a demonstration of wrestlers, jugglers, acrobats, and contortionists that the Soviets put on in the camp and sat through speeches in Russian, probably about the glories of Marxism and the heroism of Comrade Stalin, not one word of which he or his buddies understood. There was an *Alice in Wonderland*, down the rabbit hole, quality to their days now.

On another occasion, Siggy, John Koot, and Hardy Bradley were ambling through the downtown and ran into some Russian soldiers who insisted that they join them on a visit to the red-light district. The three Americans were shocked by the sight of the women—many covered with open sores, all of them smelling as if they hadn't bathed in a month, their faces plastered with cheap cosmetics. "It didn't seem to bother the Russians a bit," Siggy wrote, but he and his two friends took the first opportunity that presented itself to disappear down an alley and hitch a ride back to camp. "Not for all the money in the world...," he wrote in his diary.

By the first week of September, American transport was on the ground regularly and those Americans who were suffering from such severe malnutrition that they couldn't walk, as well as the obvious T.B. cases, were being evacuated. Siggy was judged to be among those in better shape and so had to wait—impatiently—but on September 10th, three weeks after the American parachutists and the first Russians had arrived from Siberia, his own slow journey home finally began. His final thought upon departure: God help our former captors. Language barrier or not, the Russians had made it boastfully clear they planned to show no mercy to the Emperor's men.

MacArthur greets Wainwright in Yokohama, Japan—their first meeting since parting on Corregidor more than three years before. (*August 31, 1945*)

—∿∿—

Siggy wasn't lucky in the ship he was placed on, the *Colbert*, for the trip from China to Okinawa, the first leg of his journey home. At first, everything was grand: the food, the showers one could take at any time of day, the comfortable bunks, the fresh clothes the newly freed men—Americans, British, Australian, and Dutch—were given. As the ship approached Okinawa, though, it ran into a typhoon. The waves smacked against the side of the rolling *Colbert*. Just as the storm was subsiding, the ship ran into a mine. "At the time I was below deck in my bunk," Siggy wrote. "The explosion brought me out of the bunk and up on deck in nothing flat." He was wearing his life jacket, but didn't even remember putting it on in the chaos. A sad sight awaited everyone. Two former POW's had been killed by the explosion, their heads all but blown off.

News both happy and sad greeted some of the men in Okinawa as everyone started to speak about their countrymen they had been imprisoned with— scattered, as they were after Bataan, to Formosa, Japan, Korea, and Manchuria—to compare notes. This is when Siggy learned of the death of his good buddy Baron Bukalevich the previous year.

The men had to be flown rather than sent by ship to their next stop, Manila, which added yet more delays to their progress home. A discouraging sight awaited them in the capital of the Philippines

after a six-hour plane ride there. The city had been
the scene of the worst urban fighting of the war in
the Pacific. It was estimated that 100,000 residents
had died during the enemy occupation and in the
street-by-street battles between the Americans and
Japanese. Not a major building or neighborhood
had been spared. The grand Manila Hotel had
been gutted by fire. Outside the city, Siggy had his
last glimpse of the remains of the battered Nichols
Air Field.

Two weeks later, Siggy, Frank Gagliardi, and
Hardy Bradley received their orders to report to the
dock to sail for Pearl Harbor, after which they would
proceed to San Francisco. The trip to Hawaii and the
departure from Hawaii took longer than expected as
there were several mechanical problems with the ship
that had to be addressed. To add to the frustration the
men felt, a storm hit as they finally neared the coast
of the United States. "The ship rocked, pitched, and
rolled. No one could get any sleep. Gagliardi, Bradley,
and I slept on deck the entire time. We used ponchos
to keep us dry." As they approached San Francisco,
the power of the storm lessened. They passed peace-
fully under the Golden Gate Bridge, causing Siggy
to reflect on his first sight of that architectural won-
der in January of 1941 as he was headed out to the
Philippines, little imagining what lay ahead. It was
November 1, 1945, now, and it would be a long time, if
ever, he thought, before he would observe the beauty
of that bridge again.

Siggy spent a few days, like almost all of the men who landed in San Francisco, at the Letterman Hospital there for a check-up and further rest. He was judged healthy enough to travel. Ten days later, he was back in New Britain.

—∿—

There are no reliable statistics concerning how many World War II veterans took their own life after returning home.

Given the distressingly high and very public rate of suicides among those who served in Vietnam, Afghanistan, and Iraq (one of whom in 2013 was Joseph Rogan's great grandson, a West Point graduate), there has long been a tendency to think that the numbers were fewer, even negligible, in the late 1940s and early 1950s, but there is no way to know if that is true. The cause of death by those who chose to end their lives was often reported in mid-century America as something other than what it was. Men drank themselves out of this life, but the word "suicide" was avoided. The stigma of self-harm was considerable, families felt ashamed, and the treatment for those experiencing what we would today call "post-traumatic stress disorder" was both psychologically and pharmacologically in its infancy.

Many men did not want their parents, wives, and children to know what they had been through. I have met families who knew their beloved grandfather

was "in the war," but never knew he had been in a
Japanese POW camp. I have read the obituaries of
men who were in the camp with my uncle, but whose
death notices make no mention of Mukden. Virginia's
husband, Edward—my father—thought talking about
his three days in a life raft after the sinking of his
escort carrier in the Pacific not quite manly. He wasn't
forthcoming when questioned. Something that must
have been deeply distressing at the time was brushed
off as not worth dwelling on. The "greatest generation"
was also the silent generation.

A nineteen-minute 1945 Army documentary,
viewable today on YouTube, states definitively that
only one percent of returning servicemen suffered
from mental disorders. The "psychoneurotic" veteran,
to use the term most often employed at the time, was
an anomaly, according to this account. Propaganda
during wartime is one thing, probably defensible in
many instances; propaganda once that war has ended,
complete with dubious statistics and a prematurely
heartening outlook, another matter entirely.

For veterans like Sigfried Schreiner, recovery became a whole other trauma to survive, and
for many (surely far more than the one percent
insisted upon by the Army), that recuperation and
readjustment proved almost as difficult in its own
way—mentally more than physically—as surviving in
Manchuria during those thirty-four awful months.

Alois and Josepha's son arrived home on
November 10th. It was a celebratory moment. A

reporter from the *Hartford Courant* came to the house to take his picture with three other former prisoners, friends of his, all in uniform, all New Britain men—Edward Konik, Louis Rio, and Salvatore Nocera—who had been in various POW camps and returned recently to the U.S. It is a profoundly odd photograph. All four are grinning broadly, just as they were expected to. No one would guess from their expressions or the staged, casual

Ex-Prisoners Of Japs In Home Reunion

New Britain, Nov. 11.—(Special.)—Staff Sergeant Siegfried A. Schreiner of 88 Ellis Street, a prisoner of the Japanese for three years and seven months, was welcomed home Sunday afternoon by three other New Britain men who also were prisoners of the Japanese and who at one time or another had been together in the same camp. Left to right: Schreiner, First Lieutenant Edward P. Konik, Corporal Louis J. Rio and Sergeant Salvatore A. Nocera. Schreiner and Konik were in the Bataan Death March. (Courant Photo.)

The *Hartford Courant*, two months after his liberation
(November 10, 1945).

posture of three of them that they had just emerged from a years-long nightmare that was beyond civilian comprehension.

Siggy, though, looks less relaxed and by far the least robust of the four. He's smiling, but his face has a strained quality. The skin around the cheeks and mouth tells its own story, even though he had gained back over the previous three months almost twenty pounds of the more than fifty he lost. His prized souvenir—the saber—rests on his knee.

If Josepha hoped that her son might come home in reasonable health, she had to adjust to a sterner reality very quickly. For one thing, the profuse sweating he had experienced at the camp started up again. His pajamas and sheets, Virginia remembered, had to be changed almost every day. No amount of healthful food brought back the vitality he had exhibited before he enlisted.

There was also a mental adjustment he had to make that proved too difficult to resolve, or not as quickly as the family hoped. He had been away for so long, living in a different universe entirely, a malevolent universe in which his well-being, even his survival, meant nothing to most of the people around him, certainly not to the Emperor's subjects who had control over his daily life, men whose brutality elicited a smoldering rage in him. He also wasn't returning to a spouse and children or even to a job that might have been held for him. The future was a total blank. And so much had changed.

His parents might have looked as he remembered them, more or less, but everything else was different. Siggy had last seen Marion when she was his nine-year-old kid sister. Now she was a stunning fifteen-year-old who could pass for eighteen, ready to date boys older than herself (much to her parents' concern and annoyance). Siggy had last seen Virginia as a nineteen-year-old not long out of high school and now she was a married woman, moving out of the house with her husband into the Loughery family's home two blocks away, at 72 Roberts Street, to make room for him. A year later she would have the first of her two children, a daughter. Life had gone on for them. The years in the life of the family between 1939 and 1945 would never be recoverable for him.

The autumn of 1945 was also the period in which veterans heard more about the fate of some of their friends who weren't coming home. Residents of every neighborhood in New Britain knew some soldier, sailor, or airman who hadn't made it. John Campbell, the fellow with whom Siggy had enlisted in 1939, killed at the age of twenty-one by enemy aircraft on the first day of the war, had already been honored with a small brick monument in the Belvidere section of town with a long list of those who lived in that neighborhood who had also served in the military. Others were gone but wouldn't have a proper grave for their families to visit, let alone a memorial. (It wouldn't be until 1948 that Baron Balukevich's body would be identified and brought home for burial in Nashua, New Hampshire.)

What was the result of this crushing emotional load? My reading of this gap in family history, the period no one really wanted to talk about except obliquely in later years, is that this is when things truly fell apart, when Siggy found it impossible to make a smooth and uncomplicated transition to civilian life and experienced a complete breakdown. There was no reason to assume that he wouldn't in time regain his full physical health, but he abruptly left Connecticut soon after that November 10, 1945, photo to check in at the Fort Devers military hospital in Massachusetts before being transferred to begin a very prolonged stay of several months at a military hospital in south Florida. The fact that he was sent so far away—to that particular facility in a warmer climate and far removed from his worried family— suggests that his collapse was anything but minor.

The Army hospital in Florida that Siggy was sent to (later designated a V.A. hospital) was located in Coral Gables and, until the war when the govern- ment took over the property, it had been the elegant, high-towered Biltmore Hotel, a luxury property opened only a few miles from Miami in 1926. It had beds for 450 patients and was by far the most comfort- able facility a veteran could have the good fortune to secure a place in. (A fair number of V.A. hospitals in the 1940s were anything but pleasant places in which to spend time.) The grounds included a golf course, and the hospital boasted the largest swimming pool in the country. Best of all, there wasn't any rushed or artificial deadline for recovery, Siggy learned. During his several months in Coral Gables, he was never pressured to leave before he felt ready to. Marion and Josepha went to Florida to see him in the spring when the government paid for the Gold Star mothers of the still-hospitalized veterans to visit their sons.

Siggy was also lucky in the psychiatrist who was assigned to his case. The World War I-era term "shell shock" had been replaced by the more appropriate term "combat stress reaction," and this man evidently understood how complex that phenomenon could be. One key element of Siggy's treatment was leading him to see that there was nothing noble about trying to pretend he hadn't been deeply scarred by what he had lived through and nothing productive in maintaining a "manly" silence about the pain and utter degradation of imprisonment.

Of course, every front-line veteran knew that most people—spouses, parents, even adult siblings, certainly one's own children, and the vast majority of society at large—did not want to hear, and surely not in anything approaching graphic detail, about the dark side of their experiences overseas. This was still the world of Ernest Hemingway's classic "Soldiers Home," his 1924 story of one man's difficulty in readjusting to civilian life and his family's inability to understand his state of mind, his numbness and drift. One 1946 Hollywood movie, the highly successful *The Best Years of Their Lives*, was a vivid narrative of how much veterans, mentally or physically disabled, had to deal with upon their return home. One disabled soldier confronts civilian life having lost both hands, another grapples with altered employment prospects and expectations, while the third has to accept that his wife has lost interest in him. Their problems are serious and not easily rectified, but the film concludes on a more-or-less upbeat note. That was the only note on which such a popular movie could end.

Even the bold John Huston, in making the Army-commissioned documentary *Let There Be Light* in 1945, which filmed veterans during their disturbing in-take interviews in the psychiatric ward of a Long Island hospital, felt the need to placate the Army by implying that recovery periods took less time than they often did—a deadline of eight or nine weeks of personal and group therapy was about right, the film's narrator sententiously informed the viewers—and by ending the film with images of healthy men ready and able to return to productive civilian lives, playing baseball, playing cards, eager to start families and hold down jobs. Nonetheless, the Army brass was squeamish when they saw Huston's film. The government prohibited its release until the 1980s. One fear was that the men who agreed to be filmed hadn't been fully cognizant of the meaning of the release forms they were signing. Another, probably larger concern was that the psychological conditions—in some cases, the total breakdown—that had brought those men to the hospital would leave a more lasting, unnerving impression on anyone who saw the film, overshadowing the narrator's bromides about their almost guaranteed quick recovery.

Learning about Siggy's diary and the vivid quality of his memories, his psychiatrist urged him to spend time with the scattered pages he had on hand and to record on paper in as much detail as he could what had happened to him and his fellow prisoners. Unlike some of his peers who preferred not to dwell on the horror of Bataan, the hell ships, and the prison camps, Siggy took to this suggestion with alacrity. Throughout that spring and summer, he worked on what became the more than 300 typed pages of his journal—pages he asked his sister to type up for him the following year.

The one thing Siggy did not care to talk about at any length with his parents, siblings, or later with his wife and children, was the time spent in the hospital.

He was well enough, though, to return to New Britain in September, 1946, when Jonathan Wainwright began his three-day tour of the state that included a visit to meet with blind World War II veterans at a convalescent home in Avon, a bucolic town north of Hartford, and a round of statewide celebrations for the much-loved general who had shared the prison-camp fate of his men on Bataan and Corregidor. A reception was held at the governor's mansion in Hartford, where three of the New Britain survivors of Bataan and the camps—Siggy, Louis Rio, and Salvatore Nocera—met Wainwright, who said all the appropriate words about their gallantry. After a year of collapse and dysfunction, at last, he was ready in the fall of 1946 to pick up the pieces of his life he had left behind in 1939. He was also asked by Virginia to be the godfather of her first-born child, Patricia, that fall.

(One wonders, though, how many of the crowds cheering General Wainwright knew of his own condition as an incurable alcoholic or the collapse and permanent hospitalization of his wife after his return? Wainwright died in 1953.)

In 1947, Virginia dutifully typed up the handwritten pages of Siggy's record of the war. By that time, Siggy was engaged in what sounds like a precise, self-defined, determined, and even exuberant program of recovery.

Athletics played a part. He swam regularly and earned his certification to work as a lifeguard. He took up gymnastics, his passion before the war, again with a vigor and concentration that surprised the family. He renewed his social life, and presumably his romantic and sexual life, as he tooled about town in the flashy yellow convertible he bought with his back pay. He had a new attitude toward school, which hadn't much interested him before the war, and he enrolled at the local four-year teachers' college, Central Connecticut State College, once he secured his high-school G.E.D. He also determined never to let his experience of the war in the Pacific fade into a past that was to be brushed aside or neatly shelved in memory, treated as an inappropriate embarrassment if one insisted on raising the topic too often.

In April, 1947, Siggy attended the second convention of a new veterans' organization, The Defenders
of Bataan and Corregidor, which was held in Boston
as a combined reunion and a check-in to see how the
former POW's were doing. The following year he
attended the third convention, held in New York City
at the Commodore Hotel; he made the train trip to the
city in the company of General Ned King, who had
ordered the surrender of American forces in Bataan
about which he felt tremendous guilt. Siggy gained
a reputation as a particularly eager member of the
group. At the fourth convention, held in Atlantic City
in 1949, he was appointed to the newly created post of
national service officer whose job was to help Gold Star
mothers in the filing of government forms to receive
their deceased sons' insurance benefits and back pay,
which had become an on-going bureaucratic problem.

The following year, at a meeting of veterans in
Hartford in January, he was elected president of the
Connecticut chapter of the organization (his friend
and fellow POW Salvatore Nocera served as record-
ing secretary), and in May he attended the national
convention once again, in Pittsburgh. The Rotary
Club in New Britain asked him to speak about Bataan
that year, the first of numerous speaking engagements
across the state in the fifties and sixties. It was a source
of frustration for Siggy and other veterans of the war
in the Pacific theater that Germany was being com-
pelled to offer financial compensation to the survivors
of the Nazi camps but no such demand was being

made against Japan. They wanted Congress lobbied to deal with that injustice.

All of this activity was taking place while Siggy was a full-time student at Central. The G.I. Bill was a godsend for millions in the transition to a new life, and Siggy took advantage of its benefits. Virginia complained that she typed so many of her brother's school papers that she should have gotten the degree. His majors were industrial arts and psychology, and his page in the 1950 CCSC yearbook suggests the persona he had cultivated since his return from Coral Gables: "sharp...yellow convertible and fashion-plate clothes... usually working on some deal... quiet and friendly... has an inquiring mind...a student of philosophy."

The future seemed more hopeful than dark now. Swimming, for that matter, turned out to be something other than just a means to bring him back to a peak of health and remake his body into the impressively taut shape he had enjoyed in his late teens. Between his sophomore and junior year at Central, he landed a summer job as a lifeguard at the White Sands beach in Old Lyme on the Connecticut shoreline. It was intended to be a paid break from school in a setting that was uncrowded, family-friendly, and restorative. It turned out to be much more than that. Lifeguarding that summer in 1948 changed Siggy's life.

One afternoon, a nine-year-old girl paddled out with her inflatable tube farther from shore than she had realized and farther than the lifeguard thought safe. He swam out to her, gently admonished the girl about her distance from the beach, and chatted with her all the way as they swam back to shore. The incautious young swimmer, Suzanne Dwyer, was utterly taken with the muscular thirty-year-old lifeguard. She was there vacationing with her four-year-old sister Heidi—and their divorced, eligible, personable, and very attractive mother, Lorraine Dwyer. She made sure her rescuer met her mother and sister. An immediate chemistry developed between the veteran of the war and current college student and the thirty-one-year-old mother of two from Hartford. They started dating. A photo from 1950, shot in the backyard on Ellis Street the day of Siggy's graduation from Central, shows Siggy standing proudly in his cap and gown, Lorraine next to him, every bit as happy and proud.

Siggy and Lorraine were married in 1951, Lorraine gave birth to a son, Christopher, and several years later Siggy adopted the two girls. It was to be a highly compatible union.

All did not go well on Ellis Street—sadly, perhaps predictably—when the time came for Siggy to tell his mother that he was courting a divorced woman with children. As a Catholic, Josepha believed her son was committing a mortal sin, jeopardizing his immortal soul, a view reinforced by conversations with the pastor at St. Peter's. The estrangement between mother and son continued for years, only gradually dwindling into what might be called a polite awkwardness. Josepha's fondness for the two girls and the boy, and eventual acceptance of Lorraine as an admirable daughter-in-law, helped in time to smooth things over, but only to a degree.

A truly close bond between Josepha and Siggy after the war just wasn't to be. Married to a man she had always found too passive, Josepha found it impossible to give up her controlling manner—and Josepha in middle age was a fiercely controlling matriarch—and her son found it impossible to accept being controlled in any way. That was the beauty of the marriage with Lorraine; she gave Siggy space to find his way, supported him in all his decisions about his career (he became a high-school teacher of industrial arts in Westport, Connecticut), and thought the world of him, as he did of her. Together they founded a travel business to afford teachers and students the opportunity for international travel at charter rates. With Educators Activities Association and on their own, they traveled extensively, especially in Europe, throughout their married years. They were the world travelers of the family.

Significantly, part of that support which Lorraine offered her husband involved Siggy's desire to speak about Bataan and Mukden in public. Though not a natural—or, even according to one daughter, a particularly good—public speaker, Siggy was happy to accept any invitation to relate his war experiences to veterans' groups and students. He enjoyed giving interviews to area newspapers. A recipient of the Bronze Star and a Purple Heart medal, an officer in the Air Force Reserve, and someone who loaned his typed journal to any scholar writing about the war, he didn't believe in a polite silence about truths that should be widely known.

As an eleven-year-old, I met him one afternoon at my grandmother's house when I was visiting her on my own, two blocks from where I lived. He had driven up to New Britain from Norwalk, where he and Lorraine resided, for a quick visit on his own. I was a little surprised by the nonchalance with which my uncle referred in passing to the war and its horrors, and not in a manner meant to shock or titillate. We somehow got onto the subject of food, and he didn't hesitate to tell me about the time (presumably at Camp O'Donnell or Cabanatuan) when he and his starving friends hadn't eaten for days and were desperate to put something in their mouths and stomachs and grabbed a handful of cold ashes from a coal fire and swallowed them by the fistful. He made a face. "They tasted awful!" he said. "And they didn't make us less hungry." I went numb at the thought. My grandmother looked unhappy that he had spoken as he did. I wasn't unhappy he had been so honest. I was impressed.

Something that was also impressive, but much harder for the family to grasp (myself included), was that his attitude toward the Japanese was more for-giving than embittered. He had no regard for the government in Tokyo that set the war in motion and sanctioned civilian atrocities, or for those officers and guards who had been needlessly brutal to their American prisoners, but his feelings for the Japanese people themselves, and those ordinary soldiers who had been pressed into service by their government, were fundamentally benevolent. The blanket anti-Japanese bigotry that was widespread in the U.S. for many years after the war was nothing he wanted any part of.

Forgiveness for what her son had endured certainly wasn't in the heart of Josepha Schreiner. When Americans started to buy Japanese cars in the 1960s, she was vocally unhappy with that development. She didn't share her son's more generous view toward anyone of Japanese descent, and she didn't understand why people, including many in her own family, didn't express the outrage she felt at the thought of Americans supporting the Japanese economy in any way. They had too much to pay for, in her mind. She was incredulous that Richard Nixon welcomed Emperor Hirohito to the White House in 1971 and that he was invited back again in 1975 for a state visit by Gerald Ford. Siggy was less distressed by that. Too much time had passed. Bitterness took too great a toll.

One episode, though, when he was in his mid-fifties, suggested that a deep-rooted anger was still buried inside the man. On a trip to Puerto Rico to celebrate their wedding anniversary, Siggy and Lorraine were accosted by three men on their way home from dinner. They demanded Siggy's wallet and watch. He came to an abrupt halt. He suddenly started screaming at them frantically—in Japanese—grabbed two of them by the ears before they could react, and began with enormous force smashing their heads together. They fell to the ground as he grabbed the third man and yanked his arm behind him, firmly breaking it. The police were called by people who heard Lorraine's screams.

Lorraine was horror-struck. For a minute, she was actually afraid her husband wasn't going to stop and was going to kill the men. She was unnerved when she told her children about it upon their return to Connecticut. It was a side of her husband he had kept carefully hidden from them, and that was the only time the family knew of when he exhibited such explosive rage.

Four years later, in 1977, Siggy decided to attend the ceremonies in the Philippines marking the 35th anniversary of the fall of Bataan. Ferdinand and Imelda Marcos hosted a reception for the American veterans in Manila attended by the American ambassador, William Sullivan; the Japanese charge d'affaires, Makoto Taniguchi; and the 150 others who had made the trip from the United States, some with their wives and adult children, and an equivalent number of Filipino veterans and their families. Suzanne accompanied her father.

On Bataan itself, the men and their families were invited to walk as far as they wanted along the same road they had been forced to march in April of 1942, the same road where they had seen men beaten and bayonetted, their bodies thrown into the brush. It was hot and suffocatingly humid, and Suzanne, thirty-eight at the time, walked for a while but soon retreated to the cool of the bus. Her father walked for a longer stretch.

She asked him then why they were there at all. Wasn't this just too painful, to be reminded of what he had suffered in that time and in the same location where it had happened? She was the one member of her family who had read his journal in its entirety and knew what he had witnessed and experienced.

"I have unfinished business in my heart and in my mind," he answered, adding nothing further to that thought.

—⟋⟍—

In 1989, accompanied by Lorraine, Siggy attended for one last time a reunion of another group he belonged to, Mukden Survivors, in Albuquerque, New Mexico. He was the only former Mukden prisoner from Connecticut still alive, but about two hundred men from across the country showed up, including Leo, the POW who had been the occasion for the beating he took when he was accused of defacing the production chart at the factory. Theirs was a brotherly reunion. That busy week entailed catching up on their lives—marriages, children, careers—over the last forty-four years, touring the Southwest, and learning more about what had been brushed under the carpet by both the Japanese and the American government. Their guest speaker was a California State University professor who was completing research on a book in part about the medical experiments performed on the POW's at the camp. Sheldon Harris's *Factories of*

*Death: Japanese Biological Warfare, 1932—1945, and the
American Cover-Up* appeared in 1994.

The following year, Siggy received a cancer diagnosis. As his condition worsened and he knew the end was near, he called Suzanne into his study one night and asked her to take charge of the pages he had written during the war and see that they weren't lost or forgotten after his passing. They meant too much to him.

Sigfried Alois Schreiner died of cancer in November, 1990, and is buried at Arlington National Cemetery. Josepha Rogan Schreiner, at the age of ninety-six, boarded a plane for the first time in her life to be present with her daughters and Siggy's family for his burial with military honors. Overcome with grief, she told Virginia, with whom she shared a hotel room that somber night in Washington, D.C., that Virginia should pray she wouldn't outlive her only son. It was an agony. It was too painful to endure. She was angry. She wept.

Josepha Rogan Schreiner died three years later at ninety-nine in the summer of 1993 in the convalescent wing of the Jerome Home in New Britain, Connecticut, and rests next to her husband, who died at ninety-two, on a gently sloping hill in St. Mary's Cemetery in the north end of town. Virginia Schreiner Loughery died in 2014 at the age of ninety-four. Marion Schreiner Kern died in 2023 at the age of ninety-three. Lorraine Schreiner died in 2016 at the age of ninety-nine.

Siggy Schreiner was seventy-two when he breathed his last.

Siggy at 14 and his cousin Joe Rogan (1932)..

END NOTE

This book is one man's story, with all the subjectivity and selectivity that such a designation implies. For that reason, I have tried to use my uncle's writings—some parts of which were written during the war (in effect, a contemporaneous diary) and some of which were written in 1946 when he was in the hospital back in the U.S.—as my primary source, and in just a very few instances have I corrected what I later learned were errors, largely errors concerning a date or the spelling of a name or the fate of an individual he knew. I have also, with one or two exceptions, omitted the names of almost all the U.S. servicemen he named of whom he was especially critical, not having any way to evaluate before publishing this account how fair or accurate his view of them was. I have also, naturally, relied on my memory of conversations with Siggy, my grandmother, my mother, Aunt Marion, and my cousins, Siggy's two daughters.

While spending time with his journal and writing *An American at War*, I delved into a few other sources, including two or three World War II POW memoirs and the principal biographies of General Douglas MacArthur and General Jonathan Wainwright, to see how Siggy's perceptions aligned with those of others. I read two historical works—*Tears in Darkness: The Story of the Bataan Death March and Its Aftermath*, the heartbreaking and definitive study of the subject, by Michael Norman and Elizabeth M. Norman, and the expertly researched *Guests of the Emperor: The Secret History of Japan's Mukden POW Camp* by Linda Goetz Holmes, though my aim at all times was that this should be the account of Sigfried Alois Schreiner, not any kind of wider study, and the hell of World War II as he experienced and remembered it. Kenneth D. Rose's *Myth and the Greatest Generation: A Social History of Americans in World* War II is an excellent work of scholarship I was pleased to come across and provides a picture of a troubled postwar America that is often overlooked in other chronicles of that period.

My thanks to John Barnett for his care and imagination in the preparation of this book for publication and the many friends in Connecticut and New York who encouraged me along the way.

My thanks, finally, to Suzanne Schreiner Murphy, Siggy's eldest daughter, for entrusting me with this project. I had known all my life that my uncle was a World War II veteran, Bataan Death March survivor, and POW in Manchuria, and, seeing him very rarely, only spoke with him about it a few times and with my grandmother on even more rare occasions. It was a complete surprise when my cousin called in 2024 to tell me that she wished me to read her father's writing about his experiences, which my mother—his sister—had typed for him in 1947. I had no notion that such a memoir existed. It was typical of my mother, not one to dwell on the past, never to have mentioned to me her brother's journal or her role in preserving it. I am glad that the pages to which he committed his memories have not been lost with the passage of time, as too many vital recollections of distressing events often are. All the men and women who served this country in a just cause deserve better than silence and oblivion.

ABOUT THE AUTHOR

John Loughery, a retired teacher, journalist, and art critic, is the author of five books, most recently *Dagger John: Archbishop John Hughes and the Making of Irish America* (Cornell University Press, 2018) and *Dorothy Day: Dissenting Voice of the American Century* (Simon & Schuster, 2020). His biography of the American artist John Sloan, *John Sloan: Painter and Rebel* (Henry Holt, 1995), was a finalist for the Pulitzer Prize in Biography. He lives in Berlin, CT.

DEATH MARCH
APRIL 1942

SA HIMPILANG DAANG-BAKAL NA ITO NG SAN FER-
NANDO, ANG MGA BIHAG NG DIGMANG KAWAL PILIPINO
AT AMERIKANO, MATAPOS PILITING MAGLAKAD MULA
BATAAN HANGGANG PAMPANGA SA PINAKA-NAKAPANG-
HIHILAKBOT NA PAGLALAKBAY SA KASAYSAYAN NG
DAIGDIG, AY SALA-SALANSANG ISINAKAY SA MGA
BAGON NG TREN NG MASAHOL PA SA MGA HAYOP.
MARAMI ANG HINDI NA NAKARATING SA PATUTU-
NGUHAN AT NANGAMATAY SA DAAN.

AT THIS RAILROAD STATION OF SAN FERNANDO, THE
FILIPINO AND AMERICAN PRISONERS OF WAR WHO HAD
BEEN MARCHED ALL THE WAY FROM BATAAN TO PAM-
PANGA, IN ONE OF THE GHASTLIEST FORCED MARCHES
IN HISTORY, WERE LOADED LIKE CATTLE ON BOXCARS,
WHERE BECAUSE EVERY COMPARTMENT WAS PACKED
TO THE LIMIT, MANY SUFFOCATED OR WERE CRUSHED
TO DEATH DURING THE TRIP TO CAPAS.